The Life and Death of Lily LaBeau

Lacy Rose Donovan

The Life and Death of Lily LaBeau

HISTRIA
A&E

Histria A&E

Las Vegas ◊ London ◊ New York ◊ Palm Beach

Published in the United States of America by
Histria Books
7181 N. Hualapai Way, Ste. 130-86
Las Vegas, NV 89166 USA
HistriaBooks.com

Histria A&E is an imprint of Histria Books dedicated to outstanding books that focus on arts and entertainment. Titles published under the imprints of Histria Books are distributed in the United States and Canada by Simon & Schuster and worldwide through Unified Book Distribution.

First Edition

Library of Congress Control Number: 2026931993

ISBN 978-1-59211-796-3 (softbound)
ISBN 978-1-59211-797-0 (eBook)

Lacy Rose Donovan

The Life and Death of Lily LaBeau

HISTRIA
A&E

Histria A&E

Las Vegas ◊ London ◊ New York ◊ Palm Beach

Published in the United States of America by
Histria Books
7181 N. Hualapai Way, Ste. 130-86
Las Vegas, NV 89166 USA
HistriaBooks.com

Histria A&E is an imprint of Histria Books dedicated to outstanding books that focus on arts and entertainment. Titles published under the imprints of Histria Books are distributed in the United States and Canada by Simon & Schuster and worldwide through Unified Book Distribution.

First Edition

Library of Congress Control Number: 2026931993

ISBN 978-1-59211-796-3 (softbound)
ISBN 978-1-59211-797-0 (eBook)

For everyone who encouraged me to keep going.

Prologue

To say that I'm hopeless would be a lie. I'm a dreamer, a believer in a utopian future, delusional in my faith and in the core goodness of humanity. But when I'm feeling really low, lost in my own emotions, being hopeless is my comforting masochistic blanket. Snuggling up with melancholy, she is my oldest lover, my faithful partner in this life. She wraps me in sorrow and bathes me in tears, finally tucking me into bed at night with my favorite foods and entertainment. It feels nice to pretend I don't care anymore. No more empathy. No more sensitive girl emotions. No more fucks left to give. Life is hard, war is inevitable, the end is nigh. There is no god, there is nothing more than this; to live is to suffer so I might as well smoke some weed.

But then, while crossing the street after a rainy day, a fucking sunset will unexpectedly catch my eye.

And make me fucking cry.

Not very nihilistic of me but that's because I'm not. I'm dark, moody, and bitter at times (mostly for the effect), but I'm actually too much of a sweetheart. Ok fine, I'm a people pleaser, co-dependent, an enabler of bad behavior with poor boundaries, and questionable friendships. Yeah, it was hard to admit at first, how easily I become enmeshed with others, entangling myself in unstable relationships with unique, strong, yet slightly toxic personalities. Characters, I call them. Who doesn't love a good character? The best characters in my opinion are usually the villains. Which makes me the willing victim, offering my neck with a saltshaker and a smile. How I love to be consumed.

Experience has shown me, optimism alone cannot feed me, fuel me, or protect me and hope is not a magical gnome who cleans my room, does my laundry and certainly does not get on the webcam and play sexy time with my online lovers. Remaining forever an ember in my heart, my precious hope blazes when given the right material to ignite, but sometimes it hides, barely able to be seen, smoldering beneath the ashes patiently waiting for me to breathe life into it once again. It will burn until it can no longer. My flaming heart of hope, my beautiful, aching, loving, forgiving, heart.

Fuck that bitch sometimes.

I wish I could say I'm less naive now, that I've grown up and no longer hope for a future where there is no war, where we come together and beat climate change, and truly love and support all our brothers and sisters, theys and thems, with universal compassion. What a tale I could tell my grandkids! What an epic narrative to be a part of. I see myself as an old lady rocking in my chair on my wrap-around porch, the sound of children playing and laughing, the smell of cooking wafting from the kitchen, surrounded by my community of gardeners, artisans, and creatives who live in harmony with the earth and not against it, and the overwhelming feeling of gratitude embodying me. We did it! We beat the bad guys! We made the world more peaceful for our children!

sigh

I wish I could say I don't believe silly stories like, I am on this planet because I'm meant to help create the new world and every dark moment and traumatic event has been to break me open so that I could let in more light, more love, more wisdom into every facet of my existence. Like, how grandiose and gross, right? What a bunch of new age crap. Sane people don't think like that. Clearly, this is a story I've latched onto because I am a traumatized person and it's easier to think that I'm part of a cosmically guided journey of growth and evolution, than to think that all the suffering, mine and the world's, has been for nothing.

Life may not be fair, but does that have to be meaningless?

I wish I could say that I don't need anyone else, a partner, community, children, and that I'm perfectly happy being alone. Which I totally am, until I'm absolutely not. After being in the adult entertainment industry for almost two decades I have found that while it is *easier* to be alone, no one will judge me, or treat me like some foreign alien, or worse be afraid of me; it *is* much more, well, lonely. I crave human touch, specifically touch that comes from a place of love and friendship, not lust or domination. My soul, begging to be seen as a whole person, to be loved for my inner and outer beauty, to be accepted as the multidimensional human I am, and not given shallow labels because it makes my existence more digestible.

Now this next paragraph, please read it in the voice of the Charlie Chaplin speech, the dictator.

"I am not oatmeal! I am a 3 Michelin starred 10 course meal! With many different flavors! Textures! And unique presentations! Those who are afraid of excitement, those who cannot palette ancient mysteries, the flavors of time, those who drown in the overflowing ocean of creativity! Those are not my people! Those are not the leaders, the lovers, the inventors of tomorrow! I am here to inspire! I am here to bring life! New ideas! I cannot allow myself to sit idly and die slowly because of someone else's fear. That which we see in others is a reflection of what exists within us. Who are you? Who do you judge? Who do you hate? There lie your answers! There lie your chains! And there, your power."

Ok, you can stop with the Charlie Chaplin voice now.

Look, I'm completely fine with the fact that some people might not like everything that's being served at my table. Taste is subjective, and I definitely have some unique flavors to me, but the hatred? The disgust? The vileness? What's up with that, people? Because I have sex with other people? Consensually? For money? Seriously!? It's my body! It's my life to live! (This is me ranting now, not Charlie Chaplin)

I just don't get it.

I wish I could say I'm not the kind of person who believes in the divinity of the yin and yang energies of the universe, and that I don't think one of the greatest expressions of love on this planet is two people coming together and committing to grow, love, and support each other side by side for as long as they both shall live. Unrealistic, of course, but so romantic.

Will it ever be possible for me to be in a healthy relationship?

I wish I could say I haven't been shown by life again and again, men are not safe, they can't be trusted, they only want one thing, and they will do whatever they must to get it. How can someone protect you, love you, evolve with you, when they are in constant stress and survival mode? How can you trust someone who is lying to themselves? And trust me, it takes one to know one. As long as we follow the scripts of society, we are all forced to lie to ourselves in some way.

Are any of us truly safe people?

I wish I could say I have no regrets, that I wouldn't change a damn thing because it made me who I am today. The suffering made me stronger, the pain made me resilient, and the heartbreak made me wiser. Every choice has been a lesson contributing to my evolution and growth. I am a warrior, ready to take on the world and fight for the rights of the weak and weary. Though I forget that most of the time I still fall into the latter category, weak and weary, beating myself up for not doing more for humanity when my account balance is -$300 and I haven't paid my cell phone bill this month. Savings? Nonexistent. Credit? Zilch. Schooling and formal training? Laughable. Close relationships? Minimal. Confidence in my ability to plan and execute for the future I dream? Still a work in progress.

But I'm gonna save the world.

I wish I could say that I simply do not give a fuck. That I'm 100% fine with being called a prostitute, a victim, a bitch, a gold digger, a waste of a life, worthless, evil… the list is endless. My job gives people license to have opinions and judgements about me, to objectify me and talk behind my back while smiling and asking for a selfie to my face. But they can, I'm still on the wrong side of societal norms. I must remain in the box I've been given or face bullying and harassment.

I hate that feeling of confinement.

I wish I could tell my fans the truth. You don't need me. You really don't. But, I am glad we've spent this time together. I've grown up with some of you. And in this time of growing up I've seen how desperately the world needs sex education. And that we could all use a little bit more self-esteem, confidence, and support of a loving community. We all do. We've been robbed of our relationship to our own bodies and pleasure, and consequently to each other. But with some practice anyone can be a skilled and knowledgeable lover.

I know, it's way easier to pay $9.99 a minute (and I promise you'll cum.)

I truly believe, that if any powerful institution really wanted to help people, for instance those with addiction, they would create free mental health services, free comprehensive sex and *pleasure* education, free reproductive healthcare for all genders, and launch a massive educational campaign on the impacts of trauma and violence on sexual expression and somatic experiencing. We are so fucked right now and collectively living in and experiencing constant stress due to the uncertainty and hostility in the world we live in.

That's traumatic.

But they don't want to help us. I believe the reason people are so vulnerable to escapism through addictions is because it's a way to take control of our captivity. We do this in our bedrooms as well, and that's completely normal, expected, and in many ways healthy. Except society is very unhealthy and there lies the disconnect. That's the area that gets people all nervous and riled up. We are adult children playing pretend trying to make sense of a world where there is none and it's only getting more extreme.

Porn is not the source of the problem but the way it's consumed is a symptom of a greater problem. Look at the types of porn that are popular, and you can see the state of the world. That doesn't make any particular genre better or worse, but it is information. And there is a difference between consumer and producer, when discussing morality issues around porn. Trust me, I will be discussing morality issues a lot, and I hope this will give you more nuance behind this career lifestyle.

Please don't take this badly, because I really do love you. You are the gift that feeds me, keeps me safe in a warm home, allows me time to travel, adventure, and the freedom to have my quarterly existential crisis I've become so accustomed to. As my fan you are always there, ready to welcome my body back with joy and pleasure, no matter the time or distance between our rendezvous and that makes me feel so safe, and secure, and when I'm feeling particularly low, it gives me a boost. But there is some really heavy shit I've never been allowed to say to you.

I've been scared to tell the whole truth.

To ruin the fantasy.

You give me praise, compliments, and we exchange such care beyond the act of sex. I feel more connected to some of your screennames than I do to my own friends. I have the ability to make in one day what takes a lot of people a week or even a month in some countries. I've worked hard to get to this point, I have put in hours, sweat, literal blood and tears, and a few ripped assholes to get to where I am now. I have earned this ease.

How can I leave that?

Especially when the real world can feel so harsh. It's a double-edged sword, ostracization from my loyal and loving fans who have literally kept me alive, or ostracization from the world around me who reminds me why I will never be good enough. I am a whore, and one who is getting older, gaining my wrinkles of experience and my skin is beginning to show the signs I live on a planet with gravity.

It's quite unnerving.

I wish I could say I didn't think about giving up so often. Especially since it feels so overly dramatic, so needless to go there, so pointless to dwell in the purgatory that is casually contemplating suicide. Because it's not even really death that I crave, I just want a break from the weight, the heaviness, the existential dread. If I were to actually admit to you the daily, hourly, minute by minute struggle I face at times to not be swallowed by the darkness would you pity me? Pity is not good for business.

Plus, no one likes an attention whore.

Do people even like regular whores these days? Is it pop, punk, anarchist or anti-feminist, to like prostitutes (or should I say escorts because that word sounds more pretty) or are we not cool again? Is Kanye still making clothes with our likeness, or has that stopped since the MAGA hat? Hard to keep track some days on what side of the line we fall on.

It's a fun novelty to talk about whores and porn stars, a far more interesting conversation than crypto or taxes but globally, even nationally, the conversation about sex and those who sell sexual services is lacking, if not completely devoid of nuance and facts. Sex workers are over here repeatedly advocating about what we need and being undermined at literally every step. Banks shutting down our accounts if they suspect we do porn. Payment processing services banning us from their site if they suspect we're using the platform to sell adult content. Email marketing services banning so many fucking words that you can't send any kind of newsletters out. Platforms that welcome us and take our money and then kick us out when they decide to "go mainstream." I'm looking at you OnlyFans, even if you went back on it, you gave us all a fucking massive scare for a few months. Although, they were not the first and definitely won't be the last.

Coming up to 17 years in this business, I can tell you, it really does get disheartening, the lack of societal support, government support, pretty much any support outside of our own industry. In my experience people don't care because of their own internalized whorephobia, projections after being brainwashed by the media- they really think they're helping us. Sometimes the hatred of sex workers stems from internal feelings of jealousy or insecurity, and we are easy scapegoats. Even some of our own, after leaving the business, begin villainizing it. Using the platforms that they received from porn to now criticize it, yet still using sex to sell their message and to continue making money.

Porn is a choice we make, but it's society that keeps us in prison. It's not porn that degrades us, it's the real world. To exist in the public sphere in the mainstream world there are lines you're not allowed to cross, if you're a woman. Basically, never be too much of anything. Too sexy, too smart, too confident, too happy, and especially too sexual unless a man has specifically asked you to be and even then, he will judge you for it. The world is changing fast and in some ways that's really promising, the younger generation seems to get it more and they are doing more therapy but they are having less sex, because they're fucking depressed, with every reason to be.

Is porn to blame?

Some people think we deserve to die for existing. Isn't that wild? The reasoning of: I have sex with multiple people, so I deserve to die. When a porn star dies the world doesn't mourn, they make jokes, or use it for PR. But the porn industry cries, each individual in their own way. There is a collective knot in our stomachs because we know the struggle, we know we are lucky to be alive, to have enough serotonin or support to make it through another day.

Why are we not allowed to be human? Would that break the balance so horribly to not have a universal scapegoat? What kind of world would that be where we all couldn't laugh at dead hooker jokes?

The horror.

The dehumanization isn't from the fans, they are more likely to "superhuman" us. See us as invincible sex idols who are better, and superior, living a life they dream, fucking anyone we choose whenever we choose and never having bad sex because we are GODS! Which is way flattering actually. Untrue but flattering.

Porn stars, sex-workers, cam-models, etc., we are just as confused and can feel just as awkward navigating the dating sphere as you non-porn folk. Sometimes even more so! People always want to know how being in the industry has affected my dating life. I will try my best to explain.

Imagine you are a professional dancer, and you've spent the last part of your life learning and perfecting certain dances. Some dances you like more than others and sometimes you have to do a dance which is not your favorite, perhaps this dance is very difficult, or physically demanding, maybe you and your dance partner don't like each other very much, but you both derive satisfaction from doing the dance as well as you can and getting a good score from the judges. You love dancing and whether it's for competition or fun, the act itself is enjoyable for you. Sure, if your partner messes up you're going to be annoyed, one day they may accidentally drop you and cause you physical harm, or on extremely rare occasions you could get paired with someone who wants to intentionally make you look bad, their own ego replacing logic. At the end you will still love to dance because dancing is part of who you are, it makes you happy, but you will learn to advocate for yourself and choose your partners more carefully. Then you retire from professional dancing, going out in the world on occasion to freestyle just for fun. Dancing with non-professionals isn't quite the same, you're not going to be able to do all the tricks and technical feats that you've learned unless by some chance the other person has taken the time to learn these things themselves. And that's ok because you're patient and you know not everyone is a professional dancer, and you really enjoy connecting with others. Now fast forward, you've found someone you love dancing with, and you both get together to do it regularly. You feel so good being around this person, safe to express yourself with your body and they seem to enjoy doing the same. But eventually they start to feel insecure, asking you if you miss the things you used to do while dancing professionally. You assure them if that was something you needed, then you would tell them and you both could discuss what that would look like. You also encourage them to take some dance classes on their own if that's something that would make them feel more confident. "Oh, but you know all about that, can't you just teach me?" they ask. And yes, technically you can, but it begins to feel like their success is your responsibility now. You kind of wish they would take some initiative on their own to surprise you with a tango or a waltz out of the blue, because you can see that the relationship is changing from partner to teacher and the power dynamics are getting a little muddy. You begin fighting more, they've put you on a pedestal and there is now a hierarchy. They start to lose interest in learning altogether since you'll always know more, and besides there's no way they'll ever catch up. They stop dancing with you as often or only want to dance the one they do really well, because they're embarrassed of their performance otherwise. This begins to feel a little repetitive for both of you. They begin looking for other dance partners who don't make them feel this way, but they don't tell you this. You just realize one day you haven't enjoyed dancing for a while because it just seems to make the situation worse. Maybe you go back for a stint here and there in the professional realm just to give it a go and have some fun, win some prizes. But when the competition is over you can't let go of this massive glaring truth that you've discovered. Which is, while dancing professionally is exciting, and fun, and more of a challenge with different rewards, there is nothing like dancing and feeling the rhythm in your body, letting loose and just grooving side by side with someone you absolutely adore. Because honestly, just being around them fills you with joy, and that's the point of dancing, To feel pleasure, to release inhibitions, to connect to yourself and with special people in your life. At times do you wish you had never become a professional dancer? Not really, you love the connection you have with your body. Do you wish more people would take dance classes? So much. And do you hold onto hope that there's someone out there who loves dancing and learning new steps as much as you?

Every single day.

When I was a teenager, I saw a documentary on Sasha Grey, I saw how my guy friends idolized her and talked about her almost with reverence and also some envy. She held their attention, got their respect even if it was hidden behind bravado and jokes. Then later when my roomie showed me some of her favorite porn, stuff by Jake Malone, Belladonna, Bobbi Starr, super hardcore fem on fem BDSM during a time when extreme was in and gonzo was all the rage. I was completely blown away. They looked so powerful, so sure of themselves, the way they talked and the way they fucked it was the epitome of power. I wanted to be like them.

I wanted to feel that power myself.

And so eventually I did, and let me tell you, it is power. Sexual knowledge and knowing one's body, being able to advocate for one's desires, knowing how to make sex a game both physical and psychological, that is fucking powerful. And I would guess, 95% of the population on this planet has no fucking clue how to tap into this, some people have never experienced pleasure at all, only fear and pain and guilt.

Call me a conspiracy theorist but I think that's by design. Not like there's an illuminati controlling everything but as the saying goes. Everything in this life is about sex, except sex, that's about power. Imagine if everyone felt good in their bodies, could access this feeling of pleasure daily, creating their own power and equipped with the knowledge of how to exchange it with another in a healthy way. Sexual interactions, based on mutual respect and reverence, instead of unconscious control and dominance.

Wouldn't that be incredible?

Advertisements are full of sexually explicit material; you can't walk down the street without seeing suggestive photos or videos selling fucking shoes or cars. The mainstream gets to use sexuality to sell you things you don't need and then shames you for being horny. I'm not saying there's something wrong with sex, I'm saying there's something wrong with hypocrisy. You're not a bad person for being horny, and I'm not a bad girl because I've had a lot of sex.

But we live in a society that is constantly contradicting itself and changing the rules to benefit the big players.

We are disempowered over and over through religion, society, government, ancestral and personal trauma, and if you don't know how to create or access your own power you will try to steal it from others. We don't get sex education and if we do, we are taught the anatomy, completely forgetting the soul, the pleasure, the play behind sex and sexuality.

There's a hole in my heart that will never fill because I fear I won't live to see a world where we, sex workers, are all protected, loved, and accepted just as we are, given resources to thrive, listened to as competent and valuable humans with wisdom and insight of this world, and importantly, allowed to work safely, legally, with rights like any other worker. Basically, treated as equals, as humans. I find that really hard to cope with and I'm not sure I want to cope with that, I can't accept it. But if you deny the truth, it doesn't make it any less true.

Why is sex seen as such a problem? Why do we have the addictions that we do? Why are we so broken? This is not a porn or sex worker issue, this is a human issue. This is a government issue, a religious issue, an oppressive and restricting and restraining issue. This is a shame issue, a trauma issue, this is a lack of emotional maturity and sex education issue. This is a communication issue, a vulnerability issue. If we can't talk about it in a nuanced way, we will never be able to work together to solve it.

The human spirit is too great and divine, it should not be compressed and mutilated in an attempt to contain it. Yet here we are, taking away healthcare for women, witnessing the destruction of the earth that has given us life for millennia, mass murders commonplace, liars and cheats and hypocrites making rules that they themselves don't, and would never dream of living by. And I am terrified. But sure, porn is the problem. Remember, what makes something taboo, also known as fun, is because it's forbidden, it's against the rules.

So imagine what would happen if the rules changed.

I am angry and quite frankly disturbed by the conversations I hear around porn and sex. The situation is unsustainable. I have a rebellious spirit, but I was raised in the same insane society as you. I know, and imagine you know too, through our lived experiences, witnessing, feeling, tasting the cracks in the facade firsthand, that something is not right.

So full of intense emotions around being a sex worker and living as a human in this society and still, I am a naive, simplistic, simp for the beauty, the divinity, and the greatness of human capabilities. How can I not have hope when I see daily the numerous unique, beautiful, original souls expressing themselves all over this planet? I tried to go straight, to be normal, think normal, give up on God and divinity, and the potential of my fellow man, and I can't.

I just fucking can't.

I think you're all so beautiful and all I want is to belong. I want to be a friend, celebrate your successes, I want to hear why you hurt, I want to know your history, the pain and the triumph of your family lineage. I want us to hold hands and cry and scream and let go of our collective suffering. I want the world and its people to heal, and I can't live in a world where that hope is not present.

It's not the videos of normal people on social media that grabs our attention. It's the ones with a palpable burning passion, the ones brave enough to stand out, the ones obsessed with a creative hobby, or dedicated to finding the truth of some seemingly small question, unrelenting in their fight for something greater, better, for progress, for equality, for the collective evolution, even for pure unfiltered entertainment. Those are the people who make us question ourselves and ask, if they can do this why can't I? If they dare, does that mean I can too? They give us hope and inspiration.

Sex workers are people who've chosen sex as their trade, hobby, passion, or vocation. This is not to be confused with victims of sex trafficking. Which is a crime against humanity and also completely and totally 110% different than consensual sex work. When I say sex worker, I am referring to an adult who's chosen through free will to consensually trade sexual services for profit or exchange of goods or services.

Why aren't we allowed to express ourselves and this trade in a multitude of ways? Why are we all required to be lumped into one category of sick, delusional, victims, without bodily autonomy or authority of our own choices? Why does slut equal bad, and not passionate?

And yet, the longer I stay in this life I've designed, I see day by day the more difficult it becomes to escape. Like the doors to freedom are closing inch by inch and I have no idea how to stop them. I tell myself, one day I'll look back and it will all be worth it. I've gone through this because I will come out the other side stronger and wiser and more able to help others. So why do I feel such a strong desire to escape, why do I feel trapped?

Have you ever looked at me or another sex worker and thought, you're better than this? She/he deserves more? Questioned or passed judgement on how many men and women I've fucked? You have every right to, but these all contribute to our chains, the weights we have to carry for you, because they're your chains too. Body count? In the hundreds. And? I wake up in the morning and have coffee just like you.

Take a moment and ask, do you *really* care about sex workers, or does it make you feel better about yourself to have a victim to look at and feel sorry for? In order to help in our liberation, I'm asking you to see us as capable and conscious humans who have been both vulnerable to circumstance and yet made choices within those parameters. The only oppressor we truly have is society, and ourselves. The only true danger we face is not being seen as valid humans with our own body autonomy and ability to consent. Everything else is subjective, has nuance, and deserves discussion as well but does not directly put us in harm like those two things do.

Every new person, every new relationship I perform the same routine. Apologizing for existing, if not outwardly than subconsciously with self-deprecating statements, the practiced look of embarrassment on my face when situations that call for truth are skillfully evaded by rehearsed answers and of course humor, or overconfidence. It's exhausting!

Can you imagine never feeling completely safe? Some of you can. Minorities can. Immigrants can. Sex workers are not the only ones who face prejudice, and that's why it's even more terrible when we are universally discriminated against. A lot of you know firsthand what that feels like and yet you contribute to our oppression, knowing full well what that does to someone, to their heart, to their mental health. We're all oppressing each other for one reason or another and it's like, does no one see the connection? We don't need you to accept our lifestyle, we need you to respect us as humans living on this planet with you that have needs and rights like any other human. A right to safety. A right to legal protection. A right to privacy. A right to freedom and happiness.

Still, the blame is not entirely on others, it never is. I can accept that it is my job to build my self-esteem, to accept my choices, to surround myself in love and choose wisely my friends and confidants. I've asked myself, am I really scared for my safety, to damage my reputation if I confidently declare my job title, or am I just too tired of answering the same questions and becoming a spectacle for some stranger yet again?

Sure, there could be situations when it's not safe to reveal my work, when it can be used as a weapon against me, but mostly, I just want people to like me and treat me normally. 95% of the time my safety is not in jeopardy, my ego is. Do I really care what people think of me; is it really an attempt to make others feel comfortable? Or am I trying to control the narrative to one that makes *me* feel comfortable? More likable? My brain is still a caveman who doesn't want to be kicked out of the tribe.

Retreating into the fantasy of my mind, meditating on the future of my dreams I remind myself, you just have to re-write the program. What does Joe Dispenza say?

"What we're conditioned to believe about ourselves, and what we're programmed to think other people think about us, affects our performance, including how successful we are."

Do you know the difference between courage and bravery? Bravery is when you are in a situation in which you must act, it's a split-second choice between do or not do, charge or retreat. People love to tell me I'm brave, I've heard it a lot and never gave it any weight. I would look at the way their eyes soften and feel the sympathy emanating from them, and I would smile politely but with a slight taste of bitterness behind my teeth. I want to tell them that I simply jumped headfirst into this work not knowing the full consequences and have been faced with many situations which demanded bravery from me.

Sometimes I didn't want to be brave, I had to be. If I break, the bully wins, and I can't let them win. The trolls, the cruel comments, the derogatory messages, the random emails calling me in so many words a worthless whore. I try to let them bounce off me, who are they anyway? But I read every comment, I see it and delete it instantly, but I feel a tinge of pain in my stomach, my heart tightens. Like a jack in the box of shame I'm reminded suddenly there are lots of people out there who take time out of their day to make someone they don't know feel bad about something because they're triggered.

Why? Why are we at this point? How did we get here? I'm tired. I'm sad. I'm lonely. And I wish I was hopeless. Fucking hope. Stupid idiotic fucking hope. I hate it. I'm stuck in an endless loop, and my muscles are cramping and my body is screaming for rest and water (metaphorically) but I can't stop. If I stop everything around me will come crashing down. They'll win, and you know what?

Fuck it.

Let them.

I quit.

I give up.

I'm done fighting.

I surrender.

Hate me, love me, adore me, glorify me, demonize me? Go ahead. I wish I could change the world, that's all I've ever wanted since I was a child. Part of growing up is realizing that I can't. I have power over me, my healing, my choices going forward, my actions and reactions. That's it. This is my story to tell, for me, for my heart, for my soul restoration and also for you. My hope is that you better understand me and people like me, and why someone might choose to be in the sex industry. And my fear? That my words will be used to further villainize the people that need love and help the most.

Courage is being afraid and doing it anyway. Knowingly walking into the burning forest, the freezing lake, taking the mission that scares you not because you have to, but because your inner compass asks you to. Something out there needs you. Bravery is born of survival, but courage is an act of strength, a belief in something greater.

This creation, every word I'm writing is an act of courage for me. To share my story, to advocate for the rights of sex workers, while the voice in my head says, who are you to dare? What do you know? Who cares about you? But that voice is the death that lives in all of us; Bluebeard, as Clarissa Pinkola Estes writes, the inner force whose only mission is to destroy, to kill hope, to drown ideas, action, and creativity with doubt and endless second guessing. It's taken me my whole life to face this murderer, to look him in the eyes and say, maybe you're right. Maybe this will kill me. Maybe it's all for nothing. But I'm going to write anyway, if only because my soul is asking me to.

At the end of my life, I will look back, and I will have regrets, I will wish I did or said many things differently. That is to be human, and as you will read, I am a very messy human, full of insecurity, trauma, and both bad decisions and spontaneous ones. My life has had twists and turns I never expected and once-in-a-lifetime moments I could never have dreamed of. I am not done growing, and I am sure I never will be. I'm probably way too much of a utopianist and err too much on the side of delusion with my optimism. But in that truth is another which I will never be able to release. I have lived, loved, seen, experienced, witnessed, cherished, explored, and adventured far too many places with a great many people, that until my dying breath, this hope will burn forever in my heart. And the fear? Do nothing, stay safe, hidden, small, never make any waves and die without allowing my soul to ever cry out in all its glory.

And we both know I can't do that.

Trigger Warning

This isn't a how-to manual for starting a career in the adult industry, nor is it a cautionary tale, an apology, or trauma porn for your entertainment. Though I have a bit of a humiliation fetish, the goal is not to make a mockery of my career, and I hope to come out of this process with as few bruises as possible. We all compartmentalize parts of ourselves for jobs and family and stresses of being alive. Sometimes these walls end up blocking us from good things along with the bad, so rigid in the rules of what's supposed to be that we don't fully embrace what actually is.

I've wanted to kill Lily LaBeau so many times throughout the years, jealous, angry, frustrated with the public expectations I set through having this alter ego and the inability to shake them. *I don't want to be sexy all the time! I don't want to be your sex therapist or even talk about sex all the time!* Though my core values are built on education, evolution, and serving the greater good, there is a part of me that just wants to be a silly garden girl and talk about TV shows and do my part in helping take care of the planet.

I've thought about it too.

How I'd kill her.

Starvation, classic me.

Go cold turkey.

I thought, I'll just be normal again. Get a real job. But how can I hide? I'm a fucking open book, heart on her sleeve kinda girl. Thinking about having to be with strangers 8 hours a day and work and interact and follow the standard social protocols and hierarchical structure while having someone police my conversations and my personal life on social media was terrifying. No thank you. I might complain but porn in comparison isn't that bad. We have freedom that some people can't imagine. The cost being societal outcasting to various degrees. It's a harsh trade off but one I will gladly continue to accept because of how much I deeply love, value, and cherish my need for freedom.

Entering the porn industry at 18 and doing that my entire adult life does not make it easy to get a normal job. I know people have done it, but I could never seem to. My resume always looked back at me mockingly, all the holes of information and lack of references staring at me. Yet I tried. The production company, the juicing business, the photography business, permaculture in Panama, becoming a yoga doula in Switzerland, I just kept traveling and moving thinking that when I found the thing meant for me it would stick, I would know it.

I started writing this book in 2017, and it took me almost 10 years to finish it. I couldn't figure out what the ending was. Every time I'd hope, this is it! My happy ending! Then it would all crumble around me, and I would again find myself starting over. This can't be the ending I'd say to myself. This can't be my big lesson after all the fucking shit I've been through? That life goes on? How boring! Since 2008 I have not lived in the same place for over a year, sometimes moving multiple times in the year. I don't know if I was running away from something or running toward something greater, though many people offered their opinions about my lifestyle.

My return to shooting movies in March of 2025 has been interesting. My agent tells me I'm a superstar and the work has been pretty steady. I'm living in this gorgeous apartment, and I wake up every day and think, *I dreamed about this,* and I feel so grateful. I am abundant, I am financially secure, though none of it came without a cost. My OnlyFans is consistently making good money, though I can't seem to find someone to shoot content for me that I actually like. Maybe I'm just dissatisfied with myself. I see the photos some companies choose and think, did you even look at these? Is this really one you think is flattering? Are y'all playing some sick joke on me or do you just not care?

Or am I too harsh?

Honestly, it's probably a bit of both. A lot of people don't care, I think they prefer young smoothed skinned women because it's easier. Unless it's a bigger company pictures are rarely edited so if you don't get the lighting right or the angels perfect, the mentality is, oh well, it's just porn. The onus of perfection is on us, the performer.

The reality is, I am aging and so far, other than getting Botox twice in my life, I'm not really interested in doing cosmetic surgery. It feels like a waste of my money and hard-earned resources and it's just fucking painful and scary! So, the result is that I have to see the unflattering angles, the wrinkles and hollows, and ways my face is changing with age with every new shoot. I feel defiant, and afraid. I just keep waiting for the work to dry up and be told: get filler or get out. Then I'll get out.

Why does the texture of my skin even fucking matter when there's genocide, fascism, and we're on the brink of a nuclear holocaust? I'm over here worrying about my fuckability and people are literally being kidnapped and murdered in the streets… of America. As I'm writing this another protester has been murdered by ICE on the streets in broad daylight, the Epstein files are slowly being released though none of the powerful are being held accountable, and it seems nothing is changing, we are all headed straight for annihilation.

Why does my story, the life of a porn star matter? Let me tell you, I've asked myself the same damn question so many times. Why does my life even matter in the grand scheme of things? Do I really serve a purpose on this planet or am I truly the waste of life and resources so many like to comment on my posts? That's what this book is about and at the end you can tell me what you think.

I am scared that this is the end of the world, and I would be so fucking pissed at myself if I didn't write down all the things I learned before we blow ourselves up. I'd like to think some school students will read this book in 2125 while writing an essay on the different social economic backgrounds of sex workers in the first part of the 2000s. This is simply a fling of rainbow-colored shit into the void that is existence attached to the hope that it will lead to a better understanding of sex workers.

I'm going to talk about some deep personal stuff, ok? We're talking sexual assault, eating disorders, abuse, family estrangement, toxic relationships, betrayal, and hitting rock bottom more times than I really ever wanted to admit out loud, but I need you to read to the end because I promise it will all make sense. It's called an arc, babe. But it's not all sexy and some of it is kind of gross. I'm going to kill some fantasies, and also most likely murder Lily LaBeau.

So, if you don't want the real stuff, the truth, and you want to live in the fantasy forever, don't read this book. You may never want to watch one of my scenes again. That's not my intention but I've seen it happen before. I get a little honest and bam, they can't watch me take it up the butt anymore, and that's really too bad. Especially if they enjoyed watching me take it up the butt before. Sadly, for some people when I become an actual human, that's just what happens.

Me being honest does not mean that I have anything against you still seeing me sexually, really, I find that flattering. It's kinda the whole point of my job. My challenge to you is realizing when you switch. When I go from being a human, to a fantasy. Then you'll be able to control and recognize when it's happening in your real life. This is what I hope to give you by pouring my little guts out on the table and dissecting them together.

What is desire?

What turns us on?

What makes a person capable of having sex with strangers for money?

And film it for the world to see?

A desire for power?

A need for freedom?

The thrill of exhibitionism?

The addictive taste of taboo?

And what makes someone want to murder a part of themselves?

Repression of desires?

Fear of others' opinions?

Resentment because of self-betrayal?

Envy of a life unlived?

Let's say for all intents and purposes from this point forward Lily LaBeau is dead. So, this person you're hearing narrate in your head, who the fuck is she? Me? I'm Lacy. I hope that's not weird. Technically I am the person who plays Lily LaBeau, but as you will soon find we are very different people. She's my best friend and my nemesis. She's Superman and I'm Clark Kent. And

I've been pouting about it for way too long. So yeah, I tried to kill her. I brought her into this world, and I can take her out.

Or more likely, she left me after years and years of abuse.

This process of life, death, and rebirth is nothing new to me, I've been in pieces since I can remember. My psyche and persona a malleable work of art that I am constantly creating and then destroying and then rebuilding. Life is not experienced individually. We are the collections of all those we interact with as well as the people that shaped them, and those who shaped them. We are our ancestors, our DNA, our familial stories and traumas. I cannot escape your view of me, nor would I dare try to change your beliefs of my chosen profession, but I can educate you how I came to be and maybe we can find some common ground.

Maria, Maria

The first glimmer of my existence on this planet began when my mother was still inside the belly of my grandmother. As women, we are born with all the eggs we will ever have and so during her pregnancy with my mom, my grandmother, Maria, was my first home. Was my spirit there then? Floating around watching what would one day be my family unfold? In many ways it would have been so beautiful. The warm Panamanian climate with its tropical jungle and lush flowers blooming everywhere, the vibrant colors and gorgeous blue sky, the smell of abundant flourishing life growing all around.

Maria was born May 25, 1928 in a church, Iglesia Santa Ana, named after Saint Anne the mother of the Virgin Mary, which when researching all this surprised me. You never think about Jesus having a grandma, do you? But even the son of God was born through humans, everyday people like you and me. I wonder if she was a nice grandma, if he was a grandma's boy? I wonder if they were close and had little inside secrets together, did she sneak him treats before dinner?

Growing up in the same village as her father, Chepo, population 1200 in the 1930s, Maria's town consisted mostly of natural fiber huts and wood buildings and a few stone churches. Seen as less important than the bustling city, it was cut off from most modern roadways until American occupation became more increased during the building of the Panama Canal; before that people there depended on the rivers and horses for transportation which caused the development to be slow preserving its natural charm and culture.

Full of multigenerational Panamanian families, Chepo and my grandmother witnessed the influx of people and commerce of the 1940s which brought with it newly constructed American-style houses. Between them the jungles were still dominating with their different types of fruit trees and vines growing everywhere, the mangoes some of the tastiest you've ever had.

Maria had met Gary as a young woman when the US Coast Guard was stationed in Panama, sent there to help guard American interests and the Panama Canal, and dare I say she was somewhat of a rebel for this. An educated woman who spoke English and came from a modest family; tensions between Panamanians and Americans had been up and down for decades and there was a growing movement of anti-American politics when they met. What is the forbidden fruit? Were they star-crossed lovers? Was it the charm and wit Gary was so good at exuding? Whatever it was, for a while it seemed to work. My mom believes these were some of the happiest times in Gary and Maria's lives.

He was an orphan, born in Leavenworth, WA January 25, 1926, who had been adopted and raised by a pastor who beat the sin out of him regularly. Before Maria, Gary had already had one wife and a child, the wife's name having previously been tattooed on his arm. That was nothing a little black ink couldn't cover up. Her name would be replaced by Maria's name, and Maria's by his next wife's and her's by the one after that.

Their first child was a boy born in Panama in 1953 and then 2 years later they had a little girl, and 2 years after that Maria would become pregnant with her third child. However, by 1957, 4 months into that third pregnancy Gary decided he wanted to move Maria and his family back to the United States asking her to give up her family, her culture, and the place she had called home her entire life. This was not a happy time for Maria, she had 2 children and early in the pregnancy had tried to abort the third because Gary was unhappy and had expressed very clearly he didn't want any more children.

Maria was the youngest daughter of 8 children, born into a catholic family, her parents first working as horse farmers and later owned a bakery. The same bakery, with dirt floors and beautiful antique furniture, the toilet a hole in the ground in the back, that very house she grew up in would be the house she spent her final days in. Was it this unsettling premonition of her tragedy that prompted Maria, a devout Catholic woman to attempt to give up her third baby? Maybe. But the village shaman's herbs did not take effect.

Gary moved his soon to be family of 5 into a home near the military base he was now stationed at in Tacoma, WA. A city which my mother to this day refuses to go to. That would be the beginning of the end for Maria and Gary. The United States in the 1950s and 60s was not a universally safe place for anyone who could be perceived as black. With her beautiful dark curly hair and toasted caramel skin it didn't matter where Maria had come from, she was not white, and neither were her children. Over time, barely 2 years after my mother's birth, Gary fell out of love and separated from Maria, leaving her to raise 3 children on her own in a foreign country where she had no family, no friends, and faced regular discrimination.

He had his sights now set on a white woman who came from a family of some means. She worked in a psychiatric hospital where they had Maria admitted because she was depressed and couldn't take care of her children- which in American English translates to Gary had left her with 3 kids and didn't want to have to pay child support anymore. She being Catholic strongly opposed divorce and held onto hope of reconciliation. After her hospitalization, Maria was forced to be on heavy medication which my mother says turned her into a living zombie. As if this wasn't cruel enough, when he decided he wanted to remarry, Gary used Maria's depression and poor mental health to have her deported from the country.

Why he did it this way I still can't wrap my head around. The story I've been told is that on my aunt's 6th birthday the "men in the white" came to the home where Maria lived while raising my mom, aunt, and uncle on her own, and forcibly took Maria from that home and from her children. My mother describes the cries and screams that Maria made as the worst sound she's ever heard. Though I've heard this story many times, tears of anger and disbelief still come to my eyes, I don't know how any mother could survive this pain.

At some point in all this Gary had her signature forged on divorce papers and not having a valid green card, Maria was then deported back to Panama. She would not see her children again for over 25 years. She would have a complete psychotic break after that and would never mentally be the same. Maria would devote her life to The Virgin Mother Mary and attend her church in Chepo every day, taken care of by her older brothers, visited often by her sisters, and loved by her community. She would be on psychiatric medication the rest of her life. And she would die at the age of 84 outliving everyone in her family except her younger brother who helped take care of her and died shortly after she did.

And Maria's 3 children? They would be moved into a new woman's home. She was a light skinned educated woman who was in essence reduced to the role of housewife with an especially large chip on her shoulder that she had no problem taking out on her 3 new stepchildren. This woman had 2 older sons, who would bestow their own sick legacy of abuse onto my mother and her sister for years beginning at 9 years old. Gary, often gone working for the military, would not be there to protect them, nor did he have any care to.

Being in WW2, the Korean conflict, and Vietnam war, Gary was the owner of a purple heart medal, he knew what it was to protect as a warrior, but he never really learned to be a good partner or father. He was a creative spirit, he would make up funny and vulgar limericks, take apart old clocks and radios so that he could restore them, he was an artist at heart who was forced to live by the rules of society at that time. His adoptive father had beaten more than sin out of him, damaging his soul, his sense of self and any willpower he had to go against the grain. Gary would play out these hurts on every woman who would fall in love with him. He would die of lung cancer, smoking cigarettes until the very end.

The thing with tragedy and trauma is that no matter how earth shattering or soul breaking the event, life makes no exceptions and continues to go on, the wheel of time always turning. And so it did. Those curly haired brown skinned babies would grow up to be adult humans with their own traumas and coping mechanisms. When they turned 18, each would subsequently be kicked out of their home, and they would all choose to follow in their father's footsteps and join the US Coast Guard. My mother tells me that this experience of being in the military was essential for giving her the routine and structure she needed to grow into an adult. She went the medical route and was a hospital corpsman for 4 years. She left the service when they asked her to go out on a navy boat for 6 months filled with sailors. After her childhood assaults, she instinctively felt this was not a safe option for a woman and decided to retire instead.

My mother, Cora, has inspired me greatly in my life. After the military she spent her 20's dancing in discos, living on communes in southern California, looking for a home and family that she could belong to, almost becoming a mom and stepmom along the way. When she met my dad, Harold, he had the same charming demeanor and wit, he was the bad boy, and many would say he was very handsome. He was a part of a big family who would eat dinner together on Sundays and spend every holiday together first at the church and then later gathered at the dinner table eating classic homemade foods like Jello salad and baked chicken. Both Harold and Cora were avid lovers of dance, my mom being a bit more technically skilled than my dad, but what my dad lacks in skill he makes up for in passion. Naturally, they met in a disco. He has described her as "the lady in the red dress." They were perfect for each other, their wounds fit perfectly together, 2 rebels without a cause with an almost pathological need to defy orders and demands. That is, until my mom unexpectedly fell pregnant.

I haven't talked about my paternal grandparents yet and it's because I really don't know as much. The happy family facade covered up many secrets. Secrets that would be buried and hidden, as if you didn't talk about them, they weren't there. Grandma Maggie was a Christian woman who believed in the sanctity of marriage. Grandpa Clyde was a stoic yet sometimes angry man who said very little but had no problem expressing his displeasure when it suddenly arose. When Grandma Maggie found out that Cora was pregnant, she insisted that she and her son get married. My mom told me she knew she was making the wrong decision, but the attraction of belonging to this seemingly loving and close family was too great. She finally had a mother, and now sister-in laws and brother in-laws, Cora's own siblings having gone off on their own paths. She finally had somewhere she could belong. And in March of 1988 my sister Orla was born.

Orla was a 10lb beautifully big boned cherub angel of a baby with a giggle that was so sweet and pure your insides would melt when you heard it. This would be the first grandbaby that Grandma Maggie could be close with as she was not able to spend much time with the 3 children of her oldest son. And so she loved Orla as much as a grandma possibly could. Grandma Maggie was a hairdresser and had a salon on the bottom floor of her home, and while my mom and dad were working, Orla would sit on the laps of the ladies getting their hair done and just be adored by all of them. At home, life was not as easy for Orla. Our dad had wanted boys and didn't know how to relate to a girl. He bought her footballs, nerf guns, and was overall too rough with her. A few times his lack of care caused her to end up in the hospital. He was never purposefully abusive, but he was careless which ended up in her being harmed.

The marriage of Harold and Cora was not a happy one. Cora had decided to give up things that no longer fit with this new role of mother that she had fully committed to, while Harold had a white-knuckle grip on his youth and not-so-metaphorically never wanted the party to end. He thought he could continue smoking weed and drinking with his buddies and his dream was to do this for the rest of his life. Yet in the summer of 1990, Cora would fall pregnant again, with me this time! This new coming addition only furthered the widening emotional gap between my parents, but they tried to make it work.

My dad has told me that he wanted to do something nice for my mom during her second pregnancy and so he helped to arrange everything so that her mother, Maria, could come and stay with them for a few months during this time. What a fucking idiot. I know he had good intentions, but who the fuck thought it was a good idea to bring a mentally unstable woman thousands of miles from her home to watch her estranged daughter have her second child? (God looks down with a smirk and winks.) Maria hadn't been back in the United States since she had been deported, her only communication with her children being handwritten letters and the occasional phone calls in that time.

But they flew her out, and it was a shit show. According to my dad, Maria seemed to have a crush on him and would flirt with him in front of my mom, if this is true it's absolutely because she was suffering from dementia already.

She would wander off and leave the house if not monitored and would constantly ask to see Gary because in her mind they were still married. My mom says she regrets never giving Maria this opportunity to speak to him and she wonders if this could have helped Maria find healing.

There were probably a lot of other things going through my mom's mind at that time like growing a child, her deteriorating relationship with my dad, and I'm sure it was extremely triggering for my mom to be around a heavily medicated shell of a woman who vaguely resembled the mother she had once known and last seen when she was 4. None of that mattered to me through and on January 20, 1991, I would come into the world a healthy 7 lb baby, one month premature, and a little blue and jaundiced but surrounded by my family and held in the arms of both my grandmas. It would be one of two times in my life that I got to meet Maria, creating this unbreakable connection to a woman I will never really know yet whose story will be a huge part of shaping my entire life.

Little Lacy

I was a loved baby, I've been told I even softened my Grandpa Clyde's hard and stiff energy. I wanted to be held constantly and was always in someone's arms during family get-togethers. The real reason they didn't put me down is because I would cry like an insane banshee and throw earth shattering temper tantrums if I didn't get the comfort I needed. I was the baby of the family, the last child to be born to my parent's generation, but I was also very sensitive, emotionally and physically. I had eczema all over my body and would end up having screaming and hitting fits when clothes or perfumes irritated my skin. My mom would beg my Grandma Maggie not to feed me Cheetos and things with food coloring, but she didn't see the harm in it and would send me home for my mom to deal with, inflamed and itchy, demonic.

I refused to take naps, hated car seats and shopping carts, and would commonly have meltdowns in stores. When I was upset, I was on the ground screaming at the top of my lungs, there was no soothing me. When sent to my room I would literally claw at the molding while being carried upstairs and once the door was shut, I would bang my head against it screaming constantly.

Even with all these behaviors my dad preferred me, because I looked more like him, I was more feminine and petite, I fit the expectation, and he never really had to deal full time with my temper tantrums because he and my mom separated when I was 2. My sister hated this and even at 5 years old understood that me being in the family meant less love and attention for her, and I didn't give a shit. I was peculiar, sensitive, and was more concerned with my near constantly overwhelmed nervous system than any humans around me.

The preferential treatment I received from my dad would never be hidden from me, everyone in my family, my mother included would say, well you know you're your dad's favorite. What a poison apple to have to choke down, with a practiced smile as if I should feel grateful. I was not the baby sister Orla had dreamed of. I hit her when I was having meltdowns. I didn't do what she wanted, and I took a lot of energy and attention from our parents. I was raised knowing I was the little shit in the house, but I didn't want to be, I didn't want to be the favorite, I didn't want to fail all my sister's expectations, I didn't want my mom to be embarrassed and enraged by me, but little baby me had a very sensitive nervous system and a big emotional heart and was surrounded by people who were not equipped to know what to do with it. They didn't even know how to take care of their own emotions.

We all tried our best.

By age 2 my mom and dad had separated and shortly thereafter my mom and her older sister Elise, would begin living together. My aunt had recently been through a divorce and had not had children of her own, and the situation seemed to suit them both. A few years after moving in together, Elise would receive an ovarian cancer diagnosis, but the sisters would remain strong together, and me and my sister would get a permanent bonus mom. Elise was feminine, artsy, and loved her two cats, Sam and Georgie. Her room was always impeccable, and she had a playful sense of humor, sometimes even joining my sister and I as we played with barbies. She was also a talented seamstress, one Christmas making me and my barbie matching pajamas, not to mention the 5 Renaissance-style dresses complete with shifts for my cousin's themed wedding! Aunt Elise, or as we called her, just "Auntie" took on more of the mother role, and my mom took on the masculine role. Auntie would read us *The Chronicles of Narnia* and other fantasy stories before bed and come up with fun crafts for us to do, and she would make us snacks when we came home from school. But, it was only my mom's cuddles that would suffice before I went to sleep. I've always been very particular about my cuddles. Particular, as in screaming and crying every night if my mom tried to cuddle my sister. Like at all. I was a greedy ass cuddle monster, and I still feel bad about this.

It was the mid 1990s and our life resembled a happy one. When I look at childhood photos, I see a typical 90s kid staring back at me. Life wasn't perfect, but it felt like a home. My sister and I could make each other laugh and loved playing together, but there has always been this underlying resentment, competition, (hatred?) we've had towards each other. Our play times never ended well, they always seemed to reach a point of no return, someone would blow up, hit, kick or slap the other, make them cry (usually me) and we'd both be sent to our room or made to be quiet for a time if we were in the car. We could never get along for an extended amount of time. My mom calls us oil and water, night and day, I call us raised in an unstable and sometimes volatile environment which pitted us against each other in an already limited emotional resource environment in order to get compliance by emotionally immature parents. Not to be a bitch or anything. I mean, aren't all our parents kind of like that?

My mom worked in administration at a hospital and my Aunt Elise worked for the *Seattle Times* newspaper. I would attend Henry David Thoreau Elementary School in Bothell WA and become best friends with the daughter of my babysitter. She was one year older than me and we would play dress up and make believe, with her favorite anime playing on the TV as our background. Her house always smelled of plastic toys and maple syrup, as most children's facilities do.

Even in kindergarten and first and second grade I knew I wanted to be a performer, writing in my diary how I wanted to be a singer and a dancer and making up songs with other little girls while dancing on that thick brown carpet of her daycare. I dreamed of being an actress and would memorize scenes from my favorite shows and movies and act them out by myself over and over. Creating alternative scenes and storylines with my favorite characters in my mind and attempting sometimes to even write my own books. The creative inspiration paired with artistic longing was… painful, even at 6.

Some of my best memories are going to Chuckanut Bay on the Puget Sound, taking a road trip to visit our half-Aunt Linda (from my Grandpa Gary's 1st marriage) in southern California at her beautiful perfectly decorated home straight out of the pages of Better Homes and Gardens, or seeing my Uncle Bob in Arizona and swimming in his pool for 8 hours a day, only getting out when the monsoons rolled in and our parents would caution us on the risk of lightning strike.

Back near our house in Bothell, Washington, we would frequent Juanita Park, and I would learn to swim at St. Edwards pool, and in the summer we would walk along the Kirkland waterfront eating ice cream. We had birthdays and holidays and work parties and camping trips and those early childhood days were really idyllic. That's childhood, you don't know any better, you've nothing to compare it to. You don't realize life's good until you have to experience it when it's not.

Though my dad was not living with us, we'd see him a few times a month. We both loved our dad, but he also scared us. When Orla and I had to spend time with him, though limited, we were never sure what the days would hold, what horror story we'd come home with, or what anxiety-inducing public embarrassment we'd have to sit through. Orla is 3 years older than me, and she would talk back, try to stand up for herself against his bad behavior. I learned to be quiet, to not make problems, to smile and be a good girl, but inside my whole body was tight, my heart afraid to even beat, so as not to set him off. My face was neutral, even happy looking, because I was just wanting his anger to go away. Oftentimes I would take on the role of mediator between him and my sister after a blowup, just wanting everyone to stop being mad at each other. She accused me of being a fence rider, angry if I didn't pick a side. This was so hard to understand as a child. He was a Disneyland Dad, who, when he wasn't angry or yelling, was actually quite fun and took us on a lot of adventures, trips and outings.

But more importantly, he was simply my dad.

I remember he had a boat for a while which had a small hole in it, and we would have to dredge the water out when out crabbing on the Puget Sound. He also had an RV and took us on camping trips to the ocean, one of my favorite memories being the time we went "snipe" hunting. For those who don't know, snipe hunting is a joke you play on kids/teenagers telling them there's an invasive species of birds in a certain park and to find them you have to shake a stick in the bushes and then catch them quickly with a sack. Supposedly the parks give you money when you turn in these birds. The goal is to make you look stupid shaking a stick in a bush and being afraid of an imaginary bird. It was a silly prank but provided hours of laughing and walking along the beach in the evening with him and my sister and my best friend Taylor. Her and I were so into it, and I was disappointed when I found out it was just a prank. I had planned my whole future and retirement around the sport 30 minutes into it.

Unfortunately, dad was good at making empty promises, downplaying the addictions that spread through every root, every branch of my paternal family tree. The message I learned from them growing up was when you're not perfect, the family will gossip behind your back. One of their favorite targets, the original scapegoat, being my dad. To be fair he made it really easy for them with his anger issues. I remember feeling so torn because I love my dad as any child would, and was equally embarrassed of his behavior, sometimes even frightened. It didn't feel right to complain so much about him and at the same time it felt amazing to be able to vent to people who understood.

After Grandma Maggie died, Orla took it the hardest. I was only 4 years old, and didn't really know this sweet plump woman the way the rest of the family did. Her memory being a smiling curly haired lady in a photo that immortalized her life but lived on the mantle, not in my memory. Her death devastated the family, she was the glue and conscious of everyone, and after she passed the dynamics changed. The kids got older. Grandpa Clyde remarried the widowed friend of Grandma Maggie's sometime later and we continued our traditions and family get-togethers, now with an extended family and a new Grandma, Deb. I have memories of lighting fireworks in the backyard of Grandpa Clyde's house on 4th of July, all the adults drunk as hell laughing, teaching us how to "safely" play with fire. One time, the tube for the mortar fell over and we all stood in the yard like crazed football players anticipating the sprints needed to avoid the multiple blasts. Everyone was terrified by the mutual realization of how bad the next 5-10 seconds could go. Talk about a family bonding moment! We were all fine.

All the men in my family are the blue-collar types, electricians, plumbers, carpenters. I have memories of them building our family cabin that sits on top of Stevens Pass which has, in my opinion, the most beautiful view in the world. We'd spend the days up there walking in the forest, or shooting rifles off the deck at different targets, safety always a strict priority. Sitting by the fire at night and looking at all the sparkling stars in the sky, river rafting trips near Lake Wenatchee that lasted all day and into the evening, throughout the years we celebrated together a countless number of birthdays and weddings, dancing drunkenly and jovially all night.

My dad's family knows how to have a good time, they love to dance, laugh, and are what one might call, happy drunks. I have warm loving and hilarious memories that I cherish, and I feel grateful for. I know that not everyone has a family like this, and it wasn't all bad, mostly it was good. Yet I'm sad that I don't know how to interact and feel at ease around my family without alcohol, and I feel guilty and ashamed knowing how much fun I do have when I say, fuck it and let myself just get drunk and be merry along with them. For a long time, I craved that closeness, like a drug. My need to be accepted, included, deemed sufficient, overpowering my need for self-respect, integrity, dignity, and autonomy.

It might not sound like it, but I love my family. I love my dad, I love when I think of his laugh, I love the way he taught me to adventure and appreciate the outdoors. I love how he was always so proud of me when I learned a new skill or the way he'd boast to others about my dedication to something I was pursuing, whether it was catching a fish or a modeling career. In my heart I know he tried, and did the best he could to be a dad. He came from his own story of trauma, and I've quietly wondered about the possibility of the men in my family being on the autistic spectrum. But no one talked about mental health back then.

I credit a lot of my humor and wit to my dad. He could make friends easily and he was always ready to help a little old lady, or stop a burglar who was running from the cops (true story), but he could also snap and go into a rage for simple accidents or mistakes. I have forgiven my dad for who he was when I was a child. I have tried to understand why he is the way he is and accept him exactly as he is now, while maintaining my own boundaries. And yet, I think there will always be a part of me that grieves for the little girl who to this day feels afraid in her own body, so scared to upset anyone as if my body remembers that it's not safe to do so.

My dad has told me that my mom required him to have supervised visits and that made it hard for him to plan time with us. My mom said it was his alcohol use that was the real culprit. I'm sure the truth is somewhere in the middle. After a while, my mom and auntie would make the choice to move from Washington to Arizona to be closer to their brother, my Uncle Bob. The year was 1999 and Y2K was the current global crisis. Going from Seattle, the land of tech millionaires, the dark moody Pacific Ocean, thick, overgrown deep emerald forests, rich hippie culture personified in one of our first major exports, Starbucks-to the dry, dusty southwest deserts, full of cowboys, saloons, cacti and brown monotone landscapes was not a thrilling thing for me and my sister. I was the opposite of Bella from Twilight.

I could sense we were different, we weren't cut from the same cowhide. Looking back, I can say I really enjoyed my childhood there and never felt my mom made a bad decision though sometimes I wonder what would have happened if we'd stayed in Washington. She always says, "If only we had gotten you into a fine art or performing arts school" and what she means is, she thinks I have a lot of artistic potential and it was wasted by moving to Payson, Arizona where there is nothing other than national forest an hour each way. Maybe then, my talents wouldn't have been wasted on porn. And she is right, in the fact that I would have had other opportunities if they had moved to a place with more resources, but I hate looking back like that. Because the reality is I loved living in Payson and think that growing up in a small town made me a kinder, more grounded person.

Personally, I loved roaming the Mogollon rim and camping at Woodscanyon Lake, especially in the fall. I took road trips to Phoenix, which we just called "the valley," with my friends for concerts or shopping, Payson didn't even have a mall. Everyone thinks the desert is just dry cactus, but we lived in the mountains. 5000 ft elevation, and there were pine trees and lakes and snow in the wintertime, blazing hot 120-degree summers, leaves changing to gold in the fall, we had it all.

There was a theater department at school, and I also started playing the flute in band in 4th grade. My mom remarried when I was around 12 and he was a super cool dude. We were merciless to him, the Sunday school teacher from our church. My dad's side of the family nicknamed him, "koom bye yah," because he played guitar and sang songs about Jesus. But you know what? I wrote a song for Jesus, and he helped me put it on guitar and we would sing it in Sunday school and it made me feel so purposeful, so proud.

I still think of that, and him when I play guitar.

He was a safe non-harmful man, no fits of rage, no addiction issues, and he knew how to be age appropriate with my sister and me. I'm really thankful he was in our lives even if I couldn't appreciate it at the time. Looking back at all the relationships with men in my life I think about the number that have been safe, *and* uninvested with sleeping with me. A handful? Less?

When my mom decided to marry Larry, it caused a rift in the relationship with my Auntie, who was still living with us at the time, and still battling ovarian cancer. To be sure, it was a very tough transition for all of us in the household. I cried so much on their wedding night. I'm not even sure I knew why I was crying, but I couldn't stop. Auntie and I had a sleepover in the living room, I think my sister was off with the guy she was dating at the time. We pulled out the sleeper sofa and Conan the Barbarian was on TV. My family loves science fiction and fantasy, I was raised on it. And that night it soothed us both, my aunt and I. She also knew that this marriage meant her life was about to change drastically as well.

In many ways during my early years, I felt closer to my aunt than my mom. She was an artist, a world traveler, she sang in a choir, she was goofy and loved to laugh. She always had an art project for us, or something girlie like doing makeup or nails together and I carry so much of her spirit in me. Perhaps I've romanticized the best parts of her, but that's what we do with the people we love who leave us too soon. We condense them down so we can carry them with us forever.

Soon after the wedding, my Aunt Elise moved to Santa Barbara, CA and in her place Orla and I got a new stepdad. You can imagine the hormonal teenage resentment we directed at the new man in the house. The marriage didn't last long, but we made some good memories as a family while it did. Larry's family welcomed my sister and me and though they were a bit eccentric they were always so kind to us.

I remember vividly when Larry gave us the news that my aunt had died. Standing in our TV room in our house in Payson the white walls, the sunlight coming in, the disbelief and the fear, the confusion, and the hole that ripped itself through the core of my body and my being. The way I felt when she was gone was a pain unlike anything I've ever experienced in my life, and one I still carry to this day. A pain you know too, if you've ever lost someone close to you. She had been a parental figure to me for 10 out of the 12 years of my life. We knew she had been sick but as a child you never really believe it's going to be the end. Her death brought with it so many changes. We lost contact with our Uncle Bob, the only family we had in Arizona, due to money disagreements around her passing.

I believe in many ways I also lost my own mother because she could not cope with her sister's death, and it caused a hardening around her already bruised and battered heart. She had to be strong; it was the only thing she knew. But as strong as she appeared, she was in so much pain. My mom and Larry soon divorced and though he was dorky and totally mismatched for her, his presence gave us a sense of family and normality.

I remember right before she died, spending time with my Aunt Elise on some family outing. She was visiting from California, and I was feeling like a bitchy teenager and not wanting to have fun. She was trying to get me to laugh and kept making jokes and I was not having it, sticking to my stubborn annoyance. And I regret that moment so much because it was one of the last memories I would make with her.

We never know when the last time we see someone will be. I have a really hard time with this fact. It's so difficult for me to stay angry at someone I care about, I hate to have unresolved arguments or conflict, and maybe I forgive too easily but I know that life is precious, people are precious, and our time on this earth is precious.

So yes, as cliche as it is for a porn star, I have daddy issues. I find men who are emotionally immature with mild to moderate addiction issues, usually really funny, and who love to have a good time. Men who want to love me but are a bit fucked up, which is perfect because I want to be the person that makes them realize that they are worth it, I am worth it. The fantasy being that we help each other be our best-selves and save each other from our demons!

But in reality, our wounds trigger, not motivate each other. I am abandoned again. Blah blah blah. It does get repetitive. The people I love and the security I seek are always just out of my reach, and I tell myself that I don't care. It doesn't bother me. I am awesome. I am successful. I am loved by millions.

And it's never enough.

I also have mommy issues and sometimes I feel like I'm completely unsure how to be a woman, what it means to love a man, how to be a healthy partner. I'm afraid of death (theirs or mine), rejection, the floor which may at any second fall out from under my feet. I don't want to be anxious, or delusional, or magicalize love and life. I want to be a healthy human, able to discuss my feelings, my hopes, my desires, and fears, calmly, with trust in the other person. But I don't trust myself to say the right thing, in the right way, and when I try, I scare the other person, or I scare myself by the intensity of my voice, my heart pounding in my chest.

I am 5 again.

And yeah, I am mad at my dad for not getting it together and living up to the things he promised us like sobriety, and accountability. I'm angry with my mom, for not getting help from all the trauma she went through and making her children have to carry it with her. And sometimes I even wallow and feel sorry for myself and I talk to my dead aunt and yell at her, demanding to know, why did you have to die and leave us with your memory like a cloud of sadness that's taken decades to lighten? Fuck I'm even mad at my grandma & grandpa, on BOTH sides. Why did you have to fuck your kids up like that? I could write an entire novel about how mad I am that they didn't fulfill the adult expectations that I now have of good and loving parental figures. But when I was a kid, I didn't know any better and honestly, I'm thankful for my childhood.

That anger, that frustration and confusion, that lack of self, sent me out into the world with a fire and a hunger to explore, to discover, to adventure, and to experience all of life. I wanted to intentionally create myself and enjoyed the process immensely. There were really no anchors telling me what I should or shouldn't do, and that freedom I've discovered is a treasure in itself. It would be another decade before I truly knew how to wield that freedom and I would hit the proverbial rock bottom a few times before life opened itself up to me. But when it finally did, it would take me on a rollercoaster ride I could never have imagined in my wildest dreams.

Not a Girl, Not Yet a Porn Star.

Throughout the years there had always been a constant stream of cats that would come into our home and eventually run away or get eaten by coyotes. Each time we lost one I would cry, but my mom insisted that cats weren't meant to be locked inside.

We also adopted 2 dogs; I named mine Amelia. I loved my girl, and I think she loved me, even though I wasn't the nicest dog mom sometimes. I didn't know any better back then, and thought the old school methods of dog punishment were the right ones. I still feel sick when I think about putting her nose in her pee after she had an accident from being cooped up inside all day. I never did it again, the act of doing so felt so wrong in the moment and any anger I had was replaced by a mix of sadness, despair... What's the word I'm looking for? A feeling of the loss of my own humanity because I knew I was hurting someone I loved?

The chore of training them was put onto me and my adolescent sister, and the internet back then wasn't like it is now. It never crossed my mind to go to the library and get a book on training dogs, or search on Google "best ways to get your dogs to stop eating our CDs or really anything left out within reach, peeing and pooping on the floor (after being left home for 6+ hours a day) or to stop them from barking at all hours of the day when they were outside in their fenced off pooped filled enclosure."

This feels eerily similar to our own upbringing. Things were never seen as a problem until they were a problem. There seemed to be a lack of foresight into life, and most decisions were reactive, not proactive. "This is just the way things are," was the motto and clearly we had it better than our parents did so they never questioned their parenting tactics. I always felt like a bad dog, waiting to get into trouble.

When the house was so messy my mom wanted to scream, that's when we were required to clean. When the dog run had so much poop in it, we could smell it as soon as we went outside then we'd be yelled at to go collect "our dog's" turds. The house we lived in was a fixer-upper that never seemed to be completely fixed. There was always an ongoing project or room that was going to happen, next year when we had more money.

But dogs don't hold grudges, they just love you and in my own capacity, I loved taking care of my Amelia. I often gave Amelia baths and after being covered in water myself, would proceed to take my own shower while she waited patiently in the tub with me. After one of these team baths, I sat in the tub with her laying in my lap the water streaming down on both of us and she fell asleep in my arms. The amount of love I felt in that moment is indescribable. This sweet innocent animal who felt so safe in my arms, my baby.

The early 2000s were also the time the emo craze was going on. I remember when I first heard the band Evanescence it was like my childhood demons were being sung to me by an angel. I was sad, angry, full of emotions, and so impatient to become an adult. The fights my mom and I would get in got increasingly more frequent and intense. She blamed my hormones and chalked it off to teenage angst.

Now I need you to prepare yourself because there is about to be a series of graphic stories involving self-harm, sexual assault, and a very melancholy teenager named Lacy, but I promise, it'll get better.

Living in a little mountain town in Arizona had its advantages. I learned to drive at 15, had my own car at 16, and 3 years before that, my sister could drive, which gave us a newfound freedom. Hauling ass down dirt back roads at night in her Dodge Stratus to go to a local bonfire where there would be beer and country music playing, complete with real cowboys and cowgirls!

We lived in Payson for a total of 8 years and eventually I stopped pushing against everything that made the southwest the southwest and I just fell in love with it instead. It was normal to take drives up to Pine or Strawberry, down to Tonto Basin or go camping in Fossil creek with friends, or go hiking in the forest. Those roads are etched in my very being, every single curve, every favorite scenic moment that swept away my sensitive heart into some imaginary story I'd create in my head.

The southwest is dreamy as fuck.

I had really great best friends and seemed to be managing the first year of high school well enough. I had found some like-minded silly girls. Girls that loved to laugh and be dramatic, who I would have sleepovers with where we would stay up all night talking about sex and boys and be just generally feral, high on sugar and soda and the possibilities for our futures. Some of my favorite school memories come from the community I had found through being in the school band and drama club.

Eighth grade was the peak of my social status in school. Some people peaked in high school, I peaked in 8th grade. I was the president of the school, probably terrible at it as I was not a morning person and often showed up late to our before school meetings. I was also on the yearbook committee and loved being able to skip classes to go take pictures and then choose the best ones for print. My biggest achievement was becoming drum major of our middle school marching band. Complete with the extra big fuzzy hat, baton, and whistle.

I really loved attending and competing in marching show competitions. There's something so inspiring about 30-60 people creating a musical masterpiece together while walking in sync and forming different shapes pictures with their bodies on the football field. Haunting, inspiring, beautiful. If you want to impress me, take me to see a Big Band, orchestra, or live music, but it must have brass.

Everything went downhill in high school.

My freshman year I had joined the cheerleading team which was really funny during halftime shows because I would be a cheerleader for most of the game, and then change into my band uniform after our cheerleading performance to do the marching band show. I was also active in drama and loved being in plays and musicals. I was naturally gifted and picked up most things very easily, but I lacked structure and would get overwhelmed often.

The relationship between my sister and I has always been strained, but the tension increased during her senior year of high school, my freshman year, when she started dating boys. It then exploded when she moved out the next year for college. I felt I lost her. This new transition felt so sudden, and I felt abandoned again. Another loss, and another big life change. At that time, I was bursting with hormones and emotions and didn't have any idea what to do with them all and she knew exactly how to press my buttons.

Our fights got so bad, I would be set off into such a negative spiral that it sometimes led to self-harm. Over the dumbest stuff too, like wearing one of her shirts. One time she got mad at me for wearing a tank top of hers I'd pulled out of the laundry basket and to get back at me said, I had sex in that shirt, knowing I'd be disgusted. I was, especially still being a virgin myself.

Enraged, I jumped out of the car in front of our house blinded with anger, but I didn't have keys to get inside. She drove off and I found a pair of scissors in the carport to get in through the window. That was the first time I cut myself. I still look at scissors differently, remembering how painful it was, in disbelief that I would do that to myself. I would tell people the four marks on my hand were from a fork fight. They believed me?

That wasn't the first time I self-harmed though, just the first time I drew blood. I think it was around 12 when I started hitting my arms and punching my thighs. Fights with my mom ended up with me feeling misunderstood and not allowed to be heard and I started hitting my arms as a way to cope. One of the worst feelings is having my intentions misunderstood or invalidated, being made into a monster when I was simply a teenager who had made a mistake. If my words couldn't express my guilt or regret, my self-flagellation would.

I remember my mom would say, don't be a victim, you're just feeling sorry for yourself. It felt like there was no way for me to prove my sincerity. I was sorry, and I also wanted to be understood. The fights would end when we were both exhausted and usually my mom would leave, make me some food and by eating it I would concede, that was the end of it. But it wasn't closure, it wasn't understanding, and the emotional pain and embarrassment for getting so upset still remained.

Already I knew this secret was something to be ashamed of and I knew from experience the limits of my mom's empathy. When asked by her how I got these really bad bruises one time, I said I accidentally hit my arm while spinning in circles at our church. She seemed skeptical but didn't question me further. When you harden your heart to your own feelings, you harden it to those of others' as well.

I still feel so ashamed that I hurt myself. It's been years now, but it's a little like alcoholism. I will always feel the need to continue to work on my triggers and coping skills and take care of myself and mental wellbeing, so I don't end up in that very reactive dark place where I'm feeling the urge to hurt myself. I have relapsed many, many times over the years. When my nervous system dysregulates so severely, the adrenaline from the pain has a calming effect. It's like a mini bomb, a reset, it soothes me like heroin, and to this day it's always there, now a tiny echo. That voice a reminder I must take care of myself.

There was too much change at once, moving away from my family and best friend, my aunt's death, 2nd divorce, sibling abandonment, budding sexuality, 9/11, the housing crash, all within a 5-year span. To top it off our house caught on fire and my mom and I were displaced because of it.

I was the only one home when it happened and was so embarrassed when the firefighters arrived. I had done dramatic make up the night before and my lips were stained red, and I had mascara under my eyes. I was wearing one of my signature old lady floral nightgowns and just kept thinking, my god, I must look ridiculous.

Even at 14, I could recognize this was my hot fireman moment. The panic and adrenaline made it easier to deal. Luckily the fire was small and after calling 911, I got the dogs out safely, putting them in one of the cars in our driveway so they wouldn't run away.

The smoke damage was really bad. My mom and I had to live in a rental provided by the insurance company while they worked on the house. At this point it was just me and her, and our fighting had reached crisis levels. She blamed my hormones, I now blame unresolved trauma and lack of emotional support, but at the time it was easier to just blame her. When I'd get mad, I would blast *I Hate Everything About You* or some other passive aggressive alternative rock song. I played the Shinedown album on repeat, Seether seemed to write lyrics that embodied exactly how I felt back then. Angry and disillusioned with the world and most of the adults in it.

God, what a little jerk I was.

I had officially entered my bad girl emo phase and like any small-town bad kid I worked at Subway and had developed a crush on one of the local bad boys. I was still a virgin and had only ever kissed one boy from church. The bad boy was cool, he smoked cigarettes, he looked straight out of an emo rock band. We went on a date one night; I lied to my mom about where I was. We started making out at the local park but the geese were extra loud that night and killing the mood, so I took him to our empty house that was still under construction.

We fooled around on the hardwood floors but never took our clothes off. Nothing compares to the hickeys left by impassioned youth who aren't gonna fuck so they just suck the horniness right out of each other with their mouths. I hate hickeys now, I think I got some PTSD from that night. The days following, I tried to cover my battle scars up with makeup and was somewhat successful but then I had to fuck it up.

Just a few days later, I made a major rookie mistake. The biggest. I thought I was going to be cool and get drunk and go see my friend after I discovered a bottle of Absolut vodka in the fridge of the rental my mom and I were at. The bottle had been gifted to my mom by her work; we didn't normally have alcohol in the house. I got a small glass and filled it a quarter of the way, waited 5 minutes and then filled it again, and again. I had no idea how to actually measure alcohol because at this point, I hadn't ever been drunk. Thank God my phone died and I couldn't get my friend to come pick me up because when my mom got home I couldn't walk, was falling into the walls, and was saying I wanted to kill myself (remember, I was super emo at the time) and being very belligerent and loud. I kept saying, "If I knew it was going to be this hard, I would have just shot myself." Not a good look. I vaguely remember this and the car ride to the hospital.

Later my mom would tell me that I was screaming the whole time, they couldn't get me to stop screaming and yelling. I can't imagine how painful that was for my mom (and embarrassing because this was where she worked), and how annoying for the rest of the hospital. I feel lucky not to remember that. But God works in mysterious ways, and that was the moment where my mom and I both had to face up to the fact, I was not well. My mental health was severely poor, and I did not have the tools needed to cope. My cries for help had gone unanswered and I guess my only solution was to psychotically scream for hours in a drunken blackout in order to be heard.

They had a psychiatrist check me out when I was coherent again, still in the hospital bed, my mouth and breath tasting like rubbing alcohol. Coming back to reality was like waking up from the worst dream ever. I'd been caught. All my secrets were out. The shame. The anger. The severe depression. The hickeys.

They explained to me that my blood alcohol level had been a dangerously high at .30. The guy interviewing me asked if I had tried to kill myself, or if when I self-harmed if that was the goal. And while the overdose was purely the result of inexperience and a genuine accident, I had been having thoughts for a long time that maybe I should just end it. I thought, sure they will be sad, but then they will get over it and their lives will be better. It seemed like they all hated me anyways, so it must be me that's the problem.

I can see now, that's the lie depression whispers at you. You hate yourself so much and you feel like such a monster, such a burden on those you love. Why can't I be nicer? Why do I get so upset? Why do I yell? I must be a bad person. They're better without me. Lies that without the proper help and support and intervention can and do kill. But no, I told him, my goal was not death when I self-harmed. It was a temporary release from the emotional pain I was in.

That hospital visit stands out as one of my top 5 most unpleasant moments of my life, even if I can't remember half of it, the shame after, the retelling of the story by my mom to others while I sat by feeling so fucking stupid. Not to mention having to reassure everyone that I was fine, and it was an accident, not to worry.

At her wits end, my mom sent me up to Washington to stay with my dad for a month or two since it was the summertime. My overdose became a thing my cousins would tease me for, in our family dumbass is a term of endearment. We laughed about it; I was commended for holding my alcohol and not puking. Eventually it stopped being brought up because it was too awkward and I realized it was more about me soothing other's discomfort.

When I came back home my mom and I were "ordered" to go to therapy together and the counseling did somewhat help our relationship. We only went twice, but I remember on the second visit we were discussing me going to see my sister in Phoenix for the weekend and how nice that was that my mom let me do that. Little did any of us know, that would be the weekend I started partying with my sister on a regular basis. This would turn out to be the best thing that could happen to my depressed little ass.

House parties and apartment parties, red cups and kegs, being scared the cops would come and feeling like a bad kid, I remember my first time drinking with my sister after "the incident" she said to me, "Promise you're not going to overdose." It made me laugh and feel invalidated all at the same time. That's what our family does, downplay serious things, and yet, it is nice to just laugh shit off sometimes. I guess the key is knowing when.

I didn't overdose that night, but I did throw up on her kitchen floor a few weekends later while I was hosting some friends from Payson. Isn't it funny how you remember what you ate when you puke from alcohol? That night I had corndogs and UV blue vodka. Just wait until I tell you about the beets incident!

You could say things were starting to go well again, I was finding a new way to bond with my sister and had a social life outside of my little town in the Arizona mountains. I was only 14 but I finally felt freedom.

But of course, there had to be just one more violent rite of passage before I could call myself a woman. The afternoon had started so nicely too. My sister and I were hanging out at her boyfriend's apartment in Phoenix, and they were making ground beef tacos. I wanted to be cool and asked if we could drink alcohol that night having redeemed myself somewhat after "the incident." Her boyfriend then made a deal with me that if I wrote his college paper, he would give me alcohol. So I did, and he kept his promise too. And in my memory my sister was just… there. Until she wasn't. She had gotten tired and gone to bed early.

It wasn't a party, I was just sleeping over because I was hanging with my sister for the weekend. It wasn't actually violent, I was just so drunk I didn't fight back, but I said no, multiple times, and tried to move him away and push him off of me but was too weak. When he was done raping me, I ended up throwing up and he got a bowl and comforted me, cuddling with me like a friend making sure I wouldn't puke again. What a fucking psychopath. And because of how intoxicated I was he actually carried me up the stairs and laid me in the bed next to my sleeping sister. But I didn't black out that night. I remember. I remember the blood in my underwear the next morning, I remember how he didn't fix my shirt correctly and my bra and strap were twisted up. I remember saying no.

I remember saying no, over and over.

I still have to justify it to myself. I said no. As a woman I think we think we're supposed to reserve that word, rape, for the more "serious" cases. Violent cases. It was such a non-thing to me, I just tucked it away, with a resigned shrug and as I talked to my best friend the next day, laughed it off as if it was no big deal. I could hear the concern in her voice when she asked me, "Are you ok?" Maybe she recognized what I could not. I told her, *Well, at least I'd gotten that over with.* We'd always dreamed about what sex would be like, laughed about how we couldn't imagine 7 inches fitting inside our bodies.

In that moment I couldn't fully comprehend that he'd taken something special from me, a moment that should have been my choice with someone I wanted to make it with. I couldn't see how it would affect me in the future and for the rest of my life. Even to this day I hate being in positions where I can't say no, the feeling of being forced to do something I don't want to do, no matter how minor the demand.

That was my first time having sex, that was how I lost my virginity. I cringe when interviewers ask me to tell them about my first time. I want to just say, I was raped by my sister's boyfriend when I was 14.

The insult added to injury? I got a B- on his college paper.

About 6 months later, she dumped him, thank God, and I finally told her what had happened. I had been nervous to tell her before because she may have not believed me, thought I was lying, or jealous, or did something to "ask for it." She had never believed I was depressed and thought I'd overexaggerated the hospital visit for attention. Instinctively I knew she could and would turn on me, especially if it was about a man. Our relationship was not always friendly and before they broke up, I was too scared to tell her.

And actually, I didn't tell her, I told her new boyfriend Tex, while we were going on a beer run during a night of partying. Have you ever done salvia? That shit is wild. Not my style much anymore. Sends you to another dimension. But we had started the night by doing individual salvia trips. One person would sit in a chair and take a huge bong rip of this disgusting herb that tastes like fish, and 15 people would be standing around you in a circle watching to see what stupid thing you would say or do.

This was the first "drug" I ever did, besides weed. My trip was fun. My sister and I were joking beforehand that it would be funny if I said it didn't work. So I sat in the chair, took a big rip, held it in, and said, "It didn't work-" Then woosh! I was in blackness floating down a black tunnel in a river like in Willy Wonka, and the river was made up of little cartoon elephants, and they were different colors for different days of the week. And when I looked to my left my sister was made up of Tuesday elephants and that was confusing to me. Why was she here?! Then I looked down and saw my legs (Wednesday and Thursday elephants) and then I saw the chair and then I remembered that I was a person who just did salvia! It was quite an experience. I drew a charcoal poster of a purple Wednesday elephant in my high school art class.

Orla's new boyfriend Tex was a high-energy, tall, lean man with dark black hair, always on the go doing something. I don't know why I confessed to him. Maybe because he and his friends were always teasing me about my first time (I lied to them and told them about the 2nd time). But fun fact, when I get suuuupper fucking high on weed I tend to spill my deepest darkest secrets. And sitting in his passenger seat cruising down the Arizona highway at night blazed out of my mind, it just came out. Honestly, I think I felt safe with him. He never sexualized me, just teased me mercilessly with all his friends like what I imagine a big brother would do. It felt appropriate.

After that party and my confession things continued as normal. My sister and I never really talked about what her ex had done. When Tex told her she called her ex and was really dramatic and yelled at him, screaming at moments. But that was it. Never asked me if I was ok. I don't know if she even fully believed me. She assumed I was doing many things for attention. Which, I mean technically I was, but I literally had cut marks into my skin when I was upset, I drank so much my blood alcohol was .3 and wanted to die at times. I didn't know what a cry for help was at that time, but I'd say those things could definitely be one, so yeah, I was seeking attention. But to her, I was again, taking attention away from her.

However, I don't blame her for her coldness to me, she was also fighting for the limited emotional resources our parents and family chose to bestow on us, based on performance, and I was always a better entertainer. That's how I survived. Our parents created this dynamic.

Luckily for me the weekend hangouts would continue, and I would keep my role as weird eccentric funny little sister and in return I could hang out with Orla's friends at her apartment in the valley. Eventually I ended up dating one of Tex's friends, Spike, and secured my position in the friend hierarchy. Although I was dating the joker of the group, he was perfect for me. Covered in tattoos, gauges in his ears and a mohawk that would constantly change colors. He was a kid at heart, but legally, and more importantly, he was an adult *with a car.*

We were only 3 years apart in age and my mom had met him and approved of the relationship. He would drive an hour and a half to Payson on Friday when I'd get out of class and we would go down to the Valley for the weekend to party. My mom had no clue about the parties, she just knew me and my sister were finally getting along. It started with keg nights and booze fests but then we all found a new activity and became fully and entirely obsessed.

RAVES

Phoenix had an amazing rave scene circa 2006/2007. I don't remember the name of the first party we went to, but I remember taking ecstasy and chewing on childrens' toys and massaging my friends and watching light shows and then being so fucking surprised when I saw the sun had come up. Where did the time go? I wanted the night and the neon lights to last forever, I was sad when reality came back.

So, this wasn't my world forever? Later, when I saw the person looking back at me in the mirror I was horrified. Who was this buggy eyed, frizzy haired, makeup smeared, pale, trembling baby goat? Why does my face look like this? What the actual fuck is my jaw doing right now? Oh, and sleep? Forget about it. The come downs sucked- but the highs!!

Depression? I can't see it, I'm too high! Pure joy? Oh, *that's* what that feels like! Loving everyone? Yes please, free hugs all around. We had a rave family. My sister, of course, was the rave mom, and her roommate Bear was the rave dad. There were between 10-20 people in our rave family, and we would do drugs and go to raves and then after party together into the next day.

Life was a rainbow all of a sudden. This was during the boom of the kandy kid era when happy hardcore and hardstyle were playing at every rave. People wore parachute pants and platform shoes and had unique individual styles, which were harder to find back then. You really had to search to put together great outfits. Everyone had a rave name. Mine was Rockstar, but then we learned there was another guy named Rockstar, so I became "girl Rockstar" and he became boy Rockstar, and the two of us laughed at our matching monikers, though secretly I didn't like him.

There was a feeling of innocence, rebellion, and family. I sound like an old person when I talk about raves. They aren't at all now what they used to be. Maybe some still hold the essence of what rave culture is about- coming together without shame and judgement to dance and celebrate life together and get into our bodies, open our minds, love each other for our individuality, explore the realms of consciousness, discuss what it means to be human.

On various drugs.

Raves were somewhat tolerated by law enforcement back then. Police would often come, but the party would continue. These were the last days of the telephone line that you would call which would give you instructions on how to get to the party that night, often deep in the Phoenix desert. When you arrived at last, you were greeted by the sounds of thumping bass. That muffed boom like a beacon saying, "you've made it to the right place." Every party had a different feeling upon entering. Magical spaces that had been transformed to elicit feelings of wonder and awe. And boy did they. I was blown away over and over by the creativity and engineering that went into each party, rave, and festival.

Designed for the party person, by the party person. Back in 2006 there were often drug awareness tents at parties where you could learn about each drug and its effects and what to do if someone was panicking or overdosing. It was really about education rather than regulation. No one knows the human body and its systems better than a raver. They can tell you what chemical is bonding to what receptor and how that affects your blood brain barrier, and if you drink orange juice before and take these supplements after you'll trip balls and have no hangover. Or like when you're too high on weed and getting dizzy you're probably low blood sugar so drink a coke, same thing after doing ecstasy, drink electrolytes not water because you've probably already drank too much water at the party and now your salts are all messed up and you need salts to retain the water in your cells.

Raves gave me community and belonging. And drugs, specifically ecstasy, brought back my joy of life. Why focus on the darkness? Life is breathtakingly beautiful and even more so on drugs. Have you ever watched the sunset high on acid? Or see another person so beautiful it melts your insides and ego, and you can't help but want to be friends? Have you ever danced so hard you felt you were connected to an amp and your body was forced to move, pulled by the electricity but still feeling it's never quite enough? You want to dance bigger and move your body in different ways, but you can't embody the pleasure the music fills your veins with.

Have you ever been so full of immense joy, yet unable to express the love and gratitude and literal ecstasy of the moment so you laugh-cry and hug your best friend and they laugh-cry with you? Or gone full goblin mode at an afterparty and witnessed the complete anarchy of social conventions. People doing drugs in bathrooms or sprawled out on the floor cuddling with others while being mesmerized by someone giving a light show with finger lights or poi balls. I loved it! I was a druggie, but a cool one, and only on the weekends.

By my junior year of high school I was losing interest in my studies and losing commonality with my peers. Soon after my sweet 16 came a present from my dad, a turquoise 1996 Chevy Blazer. It didn't have AC, and when it got too hot the windows got stuck, but I learned to love to sweat. Arizona summers with no AC were no joke, but I didn't care. Another tool in my freedom arsenal, taking me wherever I wanted to go.

I had a taste of the real world, and now my own car, and I was hungry for more. The techno music never ended. Even when I was home in Payson for the week, I would play happy hardcore and hardstyle every chance I got. There was no one guiding me and I was bored by the social structures of Payson. Most of my life I had been a good student, but I just didn't care anymore.

We all can look back and think of things we wish we had done differently, and we may say, but it made me who I am, this is what I learned from it. But there's a few moments that you look back on and think, that was a bad move and I wish I hadn't done it. One of those mistakes I made was during my sophomore year when I convinced my mom to let me be homeschooled with an online schooling platform. I began failing almost every class immediately.

Sometimes I wonder if I could have managed to stay in high school longer, gone to prom, graduated with my class, if I had had more focus and a little more guidance, would I still have gotten into porn at 18? There's so many teenage experiences I had to forfeit because I started sex work so early in my life. Looking back, I'm pretty sure I've always had ADHD and when the demands of school became greater and I couldn't just "wing" it easily I got more and more discouraged.

To be fair, I earnestly thought I could be self-managed enough to focus on going online everyday but I would usually end up at my friend's house, who had convinced her parents to let her do the same, and we would hang out in her jacuzzi and smoke cigarettes and talk about different bands and boys. Or we would get in one of our cars and go around town to our favorite spots like the skate park or those special hideaways you only seem to find when you're a teenager.

In many ways, small town life in the mountains was perfect for me and I wish I had remained in high school, for the experience and to further my creative and life skills. I loved all the extracurriculars and I think they were good outlets for my feelings. Instead, I was determined to grow up too fast.

I felt like I couldn't fit in one box, and I didn't have a clear sense of self. Back then I thought I was a cute, original, "weirdo" that nobody could understand because I was just so paradoxical and different. The mountain girl, raver on the weekends, the little sister, and the girlfriend, the party friend, the cheerleader and band geek, the drama student who couldn't quite figure out her own role.

All with the sunny, hot, dusty backdrop of Arizona as my stage. The desert builds a certain kind of person, and it has a specific spiritual energy. You've never seen a sunset if you haven't seen one in the Phoenix valley on an evening in summer. I spent so much time driving around that valley, into its mountains, along its rivers, hiking, camping, kayaking. We mastered the art of staying cool and knew where every watering hole was, or we would find ourselves standing around man-made ones with a red cup in hand drinking warm beer, the smell of chlorine and sunscreen in the air. I lovingly considered myself a desert rat, a creature of the earth, I felt connected to the energies and spirits of the natives and early settlers as well as the plants and rocks and sky.

Many of my fondest memories are from the POV of a car. I love that feeling, staring into the unknown, a great adventure laid out before you, the excitement and just behind it the wonder and terror of being out of control, knowing no matter what happens, it will be worth it.

But every Sunday I returned home to my house in Payson. I had tasted too much freedom, and now it felt like the people, places, and activities that were so familiar before, became mundane, boring, and monotonous. I had seen a world colored in rainbows, yet was not old enough yet to escape this little town still stuck in sepia, though I kept trying. The golden hour of our little rave family didn't last and eventually people moved away or went to rehab, or just left the scene.

Spike and I broke up when I found out he was cheating on me with some married woman from his work. He'd given me HPV which at 15 was a shock to find out. Though the virus wasn't life threatening and cleared after a few months, the feeling of betrayal lasted.

The best way to get over heartbreak is to find another guy, isn't that what they say? Months later on one of my trips to visit my sister I met a handsome

Croatian man. He and I started flirting immediately and pretty soon he was my new boyfriend. This was a huge moment in my personal evolution because soon after this serendipitous meeting my sister had to give up her apartment in Phoenix and decided to move back to Washington state to live with our dad.

She was gone, but my days partying in Phoenix were far from over. I was welcomed, through my new boyfriend, into this amazing group of international students who were attending ASU. It was a small group at first, The Internationals, they called themselves. A Croatian, a Serbian, an Albanian (yes, they made jokes about hating each other), 3 Germans, a Spaniard, 2 Kuwaitis, and one guy from Indonesia. It was quite the mix, but all of them were 18-20 so could not legally drink in the US.

Coming from Europe and different countries they were already seasoned drinkers and so we would have little weekend house parties and play Garage Band. I loved being the American in the group. I loved their open mindedness, world views, and sense of humor.

I'd become really close with one of the German girls, we bonded because we both loved to get really fucked up on drugs and she wasn't afraid of my raver side as the others were. I loved doing drugs and could handle quite a bit. I was scared this friend would take too much so I always made sure to share with her so we could both survive. For most of "the internationals," drinking was cool, but drugs were too much. They were super tolerant though.

Now working at the front desk at a gym in Payson (I got fired from Subway because I didn't show up to work after my OD), and having my own car, I was developing my own social life outside of my sister, and it felt amazing. At home things with my mom were tense, even after the 2 therapy sessions, I was failing in school and mostly communicated through screaming, the primal scream of a young woman begging to be let out into the world. It didn't help that I was also coming home from binge drinking and doing drugs most weekends which contributed to my fragile emotional state.

I was a ragey bitch…

The Beginning of the End

In the year 2008, my mom started dating a new guy, some flame from her youth, and he came to stay with us for a while. He spoke Spanish, which was really helpful because he, my mom, his son who was my age, and my German cousin who was in her 20s, all decided to take a trip to Panama to see Grandma Maria and meet our extended family. This was the first time I had ever left the country, but getting my passport was the biggest blessing I could've ever imagined.

I couldn't begin to comprehend the doors it would open.

Panama, where our story began, marked the beginning of my love of travel, my taste for adventure and exploration of uncharted territories and different cultures. We had an uncle come pick us up in Panama City and on the way to the village we were stopped by police. Our Uncle said to stay in the car, and he went and talked to them. You could feel the tension, but he paid them some money which seemed to satisfy them. We would make it safely and when we arrived, we were greeted by beautiful modest homes that looked straight out of the 1950s. Surrounded by jungle, it didn't feel oppressive, it felt lush, ripe, and gorgeous. I was not on drugs and yet I was taken aback by the beauty, even if my black haired, black eyeliner wearing self couldn't show it.

We were too busy to be in shock, Uncle Pedro was our guide and showed us the best rivers to swim in, promising no alligators, showed us the best fruit to eat and cooked us arroz con pollo with plantains fried in Coca Cola. Auntie Pedro was a sweet woman as well, I remember she mended a rip I had in one of my skirts and taught us how to say "lizard" in Spanish. There were always lizards on the wall at night, inside and out because they would leave the front doors open all evening, it being a steady 85 degrees.

Sitting in my grandmother's house, a refurbished bakery that her family used to own, that had rugs on a nicely swept dirt floor, and antique furniture and photos, I remember looking at the woman who I had seen in the pictures and being so curious. There was love of course, but she was suffering from dementia and her memories were scattered. She told us a lovely story about how her dad had raised horses before, and they had a big farm (which Pedro would point out later).

There were hibiscus plants and flowering tropical beauties everywhere and the houses looked like relics preserved from the past, which they technically were. Leftover from the American occupation in the country. We were a curious sight for the villagers because this was not a place that got white visitors often. We would walk to the little bodega in the center of the village and my favorite thing to eat was the plastic cups of ceviche with fried plantain chips.

In the evenings the adults would sit outside, and I would talk to the other boy that had been traveling with us. The accommodations at my aunt and uncle's house were extremely modest and looked antique but they were clean and did the job. My German cousin was also with us, the daughter of my mom's brother's first marriage, and she would entertain herself by learning Spanish and asking questions a 20 something would think to ask. I have always thought she is, like, the coolest person ever. Maybe that's another part of where my love of Europeans comes from.

The mayor invited us to his home one night and talked about the history of the town. Sadly, I don't remember much of it. It was such a feeling of being swept away into another world. It was so different, a bit dangerous, and there were so many new flavors and smells and sights. I played it cool, externally I was probably complaining a lot, but inside I was overwhelmed by the whole thing. Fascinated, terrified, along for the ride. I was completely out of my comfort zone, but also felt so happy and free and like I could actually be just a teenager. The love of a long-lost family in the most beautiful environment possible, paired with fascinating stories and rich cultural history was everything I didn't know I needed.

The last few days of the trip we stayed with my Aunt Theresa. A petite yet feisty woman who loved bull fights, her late husband, and God. She had an estate caretaker and long-term friend who helped her manage her property as she was getting up into her 80's. Theresa and the caretaker both lived close to the water in an area farther from the city yet not as far as Chepo, and it was paradise. The tropical destination of my fucking dreams had come alive, and I was completely engulfed by it.

This trip was also when I found out I had herpes. Literally. The stress of the trip, traveling, and foreign food had caused my face to look as though I had a sunburn peeling all over the lower half of it. I refused to believe it then, as the presentation didn't look like a cold sore. Luckily, I was able to cover it mostly with makeup, but my mom kept saying, you know when I first had an outbreak as a kid it was like that. Damn her being right, I didn't want to accept it. With my womanly breasts came my womanly shame for having a common virus given to me, unknowingly, by my mother when she had an outbreak at some point in our years together.

Así es la vida

When we came home the expectation of staying in touch with this new-found family was something we wanted. But with time it became clear, we were vastly different people with separate lives and cultures. They also didn't have social media. My mom would continue to talk to my Aunt Theresa and ask for news about my grandmother and she would be told she is being taken care of and well. After many years I think I realized that this trip was not about a new beginning, but a chance to say goodbye.

The maiden, the mother, and the crone all together one last time.

Our family in Panama slowly faded to the distant memories they had been before, though the love and pull of Panama would stay with me. I am haunted by its beauty, the sadness of its story, my grandmother's story, and the resilience of the Panamanian people. The culture, the social customs, the nature, everything about Panama brings my heart alive, and I'm sure that love is encoded in my DNA. But I lived in America, I was still in high school, and my attention was quickly pulled to other teenage matters.

↔

In the years prior to this I had entered my first beauty pageant. This particular pageant was a very family-friendly and age appropriate, not allowing the girls to wear make-up under a certain age. I placed 3rd my first year and had really enjoyed the experience, though if you were a fly on the wall you'd see a girl having multiple meltdowns and fits of emotional stress between the events while her mom tried to get her to eat something between sobs while being screamed at by the person she was trying to help. It wouldn't look like someone who was happy, but I was.

The next year I tried again, this time being in an age bracket where they allowed the girls to wear makeup. In the pageant world there is a certain culture and expectation, of your attitude, your dress and the way you speak and present yourself. I knew I was being judged, literally, on many different factors. I loved the elegance of it, I loved the community and camaraderie we all shared during the weekend of the pageant and enjoyed entering the additional competitions like talent, sportswear, and most photogenic. I didn't win any of them.

The second year was fun, but I was more disassociated. Having now experienced more of life, acting like an innocent young woman with all the other pure hearted innocent young women felt a little disingenuous. When I placed third again, I decided I was done with this particular pageant and had my eyes set on something a little glitzier and more glamorous, the Miss Arizona Teen USA pageant. The costs were greater but so was the prestige. I felt like I was allowed to look like a woman, a sexy yet conservative woman.

I could never seem to dress appropriately and my last-minute changes were usually self-sabotage and stress in disguise. During the interview portion I wore a silk backless (and braless) vacation dress, I just felt so beautiful in it. But I realized I did not have the confidence outside of the hotel room as I did while staring in the mirror that morning. All the girls in their tailored business suits while my titties jiggled freely in the breeze. I also decided to wear an adorable one piece 50's style swimsuit for the bikini section because I felt so cute in it and thought it matched my personal style. I was the only one wearing a one-piece swimsuit.

I did not place in the competition. I did win best eveningwear, which is still pretty good, but for me it didn't matter, I hadn't placed, I had failed. The silver lining was that during the weekend there had been a sort of cattle call asking all of the girls in the pageant over 5' 7" if any of them wanted to be NY fashion models.

Of course, I fucking said yes!

The pageant was in September. Soon after, we were sitting with a modeling agency in Phoenix, Arizona and they were arranging photoshoots for us and preparing 15 girls to travel to NYC to meet with agencies there. My mom came with me to New York the first time and after seeing 33 agencies, I had offers from 2, and by mid-October I was flying out to New York, again with my mom and moving into a model apartment for 3 months. I was so fucking happy. This was it! Freedom! Adulthood! I was going to be a famous model and live in New York City! I didn't think much further than that.

It just so happened we had a family friend in Brooklyn who was a photographer and wonderful person. It was nice knowing there was someone close that I could turn to if I needed help. I was able to stay somewhat busy those 3 months. I did fashion shows, my favorite being one where my outfit was made of chocolate, I wore a Lara Croft design, chocolate gun and everything. I went on go-sees to different fashion houses, walking completely across Manhattan in my faux suede black boots. Smoking cigarettes bummed from other models on the stoops in front of brick buildings. I was living the life that is meant to be lived in New York. Fashion, warehouses, designers, luxury. But I couldn't even make enough money to afford the $1000 per month rent in the 600sq ft. 8 bed model apartment they had jammed us in.

Tempers were hot in that apartment. We were all hypoglycemic, struggling financially, with our individual body image issues, competing for the latest hottest jobs. One of the models was a southern Christian girl who was dating some guy from the south and would get into screaming matches with him regularly on the phone. We all listened on the other side of the bed sheet that separated us. There was the scam artist who was staying there for a while and also working as a booker for the agency. She ruined my faux suede leather boots after she borrowed them, and that was the final straw. I complained to my mom about this woman frequently as she stoked a lot of tension in the house by borrowing from us and promising jobs (that didn't exist).

My mom Googled her name and a nickname that she had referred to herself by and wouldn't you know, there were like 3 different sites devoted to warning people about her being a known scam artist with her mugshot and different names and aliases. How my mother found this is fucking crazy, but we had complained to the agency prior, and they had done nothing. So, we then sent them this new information. She quickly left the model apartment and soon after, I did too. New York was hard for me, I was fat. For model standards. 34, 24, 34 was the biggest you could be, but they preferred even smaller in reality. I think I was like 34, 26, 36, pretty much what I am now and have almost always been and I wasn't that motivated to exercise every day and be super skinny. The method I had been taught by some of the girls was to just starve all day and then eat home baked chocolate chip cookies with your girlfriends while you smoked a blunt at night. And smoke cigarettes. It seemed to work.

Everything was about being skinny. My arms looked fat in this position, my face looked chubby in this angle, my proportions were not correct. I tried my best to exercise and eat healthy when I ate at all, but I could never slim down enough to be a real NYC model and I wasn't that good at being anorexic yet.

Those 3 months in New York were iconic and perfect. The sweet Christian girl I had befriended had a wild side, one of my favorite memories being after finishing a liquor event we were models at, she stole 2 glasses of tequila, with ice, to take on the subway train. We were already drunk, but she didn't seem to think it was a big deal and it wasn't. We would go on adventures to Brooklyn together to buy a $20 bag of weed and blunt wraps for our evening ritual, and when a friend came to visit we did all the cheap touristy sightseeing things we could do being underage. I had my New York experience, I lived on the edge of Battery Park, I felt that vibe, and it was a good vibe. But it wasn't my forever vibe. No, I said goodbye to that particular concrete jungle and hello to the future I felt still calling me.

When I came back to Arizona my mom informed me that she would be moving to Washington to be near my sister who was now pregnant with her first child, and that she had given away my dog, Amelia, because I was never home and she was tired of the burden of having a dog. The other dog that belonged to my sister had run away a few months prior.

Other friends have told me stories of traveling with their dogs and taking them when they left home and honestly, I don't think I was mature enough at 18 to have been able to do that. But there was no goodbye, no discussion, no time to mentally prepare. My mom was right, I hadn't been home much in the past few years and when I was home, I often took Amelia for granted and probably could have thrown a ball more often or taken her for walks more regularly. I know Amelia was better off living in a family that could show her more attention, but part of me didn't fully believe my mom was telling the truth. What if she had just surrendered her to the shelter? What if she didn't get adopted and was put down? I was given no choice but to trust what she said, that Amelia was adopted by a nice older couple, but I wish I could have been involved in the process. To know for sure that she was loved and safe in her new home.

Amelia and I were on new different paths, both in unfamiliar territory and having to learn a new way to survive. I hope the rest of her life was happy, peaceful, and full of love and I wish I had been more present and cherished the time we had together more. This is a repeated lesson in my life, always so busy focusing on the future that I forget to live in the now.

It will take me many years to fully understand this.

The Glory(hole) Days

People ask me what advice I have for people thinking about getting into the porn industry. Looking back, it's painful all the mistakes I made. I wish I could have done so many things differently. I cringe when I think of how my insecurities sabotaged me over and over again.

It takes incredible resilience to be in the adult industry. Physically, yes. But emotionally, more. Having multiple partners that we share the physical act with without having emotional connection or attachment to; or the degrading circumstances and explicit acts coerced out of us in the heat of the moment forever immortalized on film, is not the thing which causes this long-term emotional stress. That's actually the fun part. It's adult playtime. It's a taboo free zone. We know the assignment. We are here to make porn.

Mental resilience is needed when the cameras turn off. The real world can be a scary place for sex workers, and navigating social situations turns into an artform. To be well known in the adult industry is to wear the scarlet "S." Publicly. Forever. No one can escape this. But some can learn how to profit off this.

The spectrum of success ranges from the girl who did porn once when she was young and is now harassed by her small-town community 15 years later for that one video, all the way to superstar mega babe who finds financial and public success and is made into a meme. She embodies the porn persona; she is what the world wants to picture when they think: Porn star. She fits the box.

The rest of us in the middle just work. The job is sex, and we do it as much or as little as our desires, energy levels, and bodies allow. Most days of the week we will be working in some way or another, there truly is no rest for the wicked. We're hustlers, baby. We pay our bills, sometimes go on vacation, and hopefully put some money away for the future. Comfortable, but perhaps not totally secure. Most of us work to survive.

I believe there is a benefit and cost to starting young. When you're young you're pliable, hot, full of energy, and usually naive. If you're smart and have a good group of people around, it's possible to gain a lot of popularity and success very quickly and capitalize off of that for years to come. On the other hand, if you don't surround yourself with good people or end up with bad actors you risk losing very formative years to predators and narcissists who are only thinking about themselves. Naturally, I had both.

If you come in a little later, you usually have more practical life skills and thus a better chance at recognizing and utilizing your resources efficiently. I personally think the sweet spot is 24-27. If you've taken care of yourself and are "fit" whatever your personal definition of that is, age doesn't actually matter you can still pass for "girl next door" if that is your wish. By this age you've likely earned a degree or had consistent employment for your adult life, so you've created a routine around productivity, and hopefully learned how to have personal boundaries.

With these qualities, you can be unstoppable. I mean just look at the success stories of some of the MILFS that have dominated the industry. They're not young naive girls, they're businesswomen. They knew how to capitalize off porn, they had a strategy coming into it and had also made money already, so they didn't need to rely on porn for survival. This of course, is generalized, maybe even romanticized because really, no one follows the same path. We each have to make our own. But each woman before us paves the way and knocks down barriers for the next generation, and I have directly benefited from amazing women creating and supporting change in the industry.

How does one decide to get into porn? Or, why does one decide to get into porn? That's the question I hear the most. Why, followed by how. Looking back, it's kind of crazy to me still the pace at which everything happened. I had just come back from NY with a newly emboldened eating disorder and a desire to do big things. I had no money other than the little bit I could scrounge up from modeling gigs here and there and when I was really desperate, I could ask my mom for a couple hundred to scrape by.

Upon my return from NY, I had just turned 18 and I was living in Arizona with 2 of my international friends, one from Kuwait, the other Indonesian.

The Internationals were my biggest supporters at that time. They were so proud of me going to NY and we had a big celebration party together when I returned home. Living with the guys worked for a time but waking up to loud morning farts every day and feeling like one of them wanted to be my dad, got old fast. My friend Nyx offered to let me live with her. I had met her at one of my first raves when I was 16, she was drawn to me by my high-pitched squeak I make while on ecstasy and I loved her alternative style, unique mentality and passionate zest for life. We'd stayed casual friends ever since.

I thought Nyx was the fucking coolest.

In 2009 she was working at a sex shop in Tempe. They had arcades, little booths you could rent and watch porn and "relieve" yourself in. When people asked Nyx what her job was, she proudly called herself a cum mopper. With her ever-changing vibrant hair colors to her incredible personal fashion style a mix between desert punk and old school raver, she knew about all the drugs, she talked about sex openly and intelligently, and was also at times a completely unhinged and feral creature. She made friends easily and ended up at wild after parties and on magical drug fueled side quests coming back with crazy stories to tell.

She could read people well and knew how to have a good time. Street smart. To me Nyx seemed more like a human-anime hybrid than a 19-year-old girl. I wanted to be like her, and I developed into the perfect sidekick. For I too, was unhinged, but in a different way and our individual styles of crazy complimented each other especially in party situations. It seemed like a natural course of action for us to move in together.

There were 3 of us in the house: me, Nyx, and her kinda boyfriend Aaron. He was a DJ and they both loved living the rave life in Phoenix. The scene was thriving. Going to parties and seeing amazing DJs was the main focus of our household.

Aaron was a long-time raver and DJ and Nyx had been in the scene for years and I benefited by being their friend. They really had amazing taste in music, and I could go along and dance my heart out, one of my favorite things. Life was great, but I was still struggling to make money with modeling and my part time gig at a luxury resale boutique in Scottsdale, and it was a constant struggle to pay all my bills. The subject of Porn was a normal part of life in our apartment. Nyx would wash her sex toys and leave them out in the open on her counter drying, in plain view for guests to see. We'd have porn often playing on the big screen TV, fully clothed like we were amateur critiques of some new indie film at Sundance.

It felt good to have that stuff normalized, there was a lightness and casual tone around sex, a celebration, even idolization. When she would show me her favorite porn videos with stars like Belladonna, Lexi Belle, Kimberly Kane, Sasha Grey, Aiden Star, Bobbi Star (all the Stars really) I would be in awe of their beauty and power. I don't think I was really even turned on sexually, I was enthralled by their energy.

Gonzo style filming where the director/camera man interacts with the girls and pretty extreme fetish was what all the cool kids were watching and this was the era of intense, animalistic, really rough hardcore scenes. The attraction wasn't watching the girl get destroyed, but the rawness and realness of it. This wasn't my father's porn (I'm assuming).

Living with Nyx was also liberating. She became like a big sister to me, and I felt like we were the perfect duo. I adored her, and she seemed to genuinely like partying and hanging out with me. That's what we did back then. We hung out, and did drugs during our time off, acid being one of our favorites, and had so much fucking fun. Our biggest concern was first, finding the perfect outfit for the next party and second scrounging up enough money for rent and bills. For the parties we had to check if it was at a warehouse or a bar because I was still only 18.

I was still trying to hustle modeling jobs anywhere I could. Working at a boutique I loved having the first pick of clothing for my shoots. Arizona was cheap at the time so somehow, I floated by. However, success was taking too long, I was tired of always scraping for money. I wanted financial security and to be able to do cool things now, I wanted to do nude modeling.

My first dip into the adult industry was through a site that offered to build, shoot, and manage solo girl, tease/non-nude websites. The idea being, starting slow and building a large fan base before offering more and more explicit acts.

Taking their word for it and not reading a damn thing on that contract, I signed on the dotted line, and they took care of everything else.

Traveling all over Phoenix sweating from the heat while baking in my Chevy Blazer. I'd shoot with them at various hotels with my sexy clothes and stripper heels shooting multiple tease photo sets and videos per day. They scheduled me to have live chats with my members, and I began learning the online adult entertainment world. Including how fucked up contracts can be. After some months I was wanting more freedom with my money, so I decided to take a job doing porn.

Being a young new model, I received many offers for adult oriented jobs, it was just a matter of selecting one. When I told my then roommate Nyx about the porn company, she told me they were reputable. I needed the rent money as the solo girl website was not offering me the riches it had promised, and I decided I was ready to give it a go. Being a porn star. Why I chose to have this experience is multilayered and complex, but on the surface, it just excited me.

For my first scene I was flown out to Miami, Florida to be a performer for a major site that was shooting scenes meant to look like a real college party turned orgy. They wanted new talent to help with the "authenticity factor." Was I nervous? A lone 18-year-old girl flying cross country to shoot porn with 5 strangers, no money or means to go home should something go awry? Sure, not a typically good start, but I landed the night before the scene and was taken to a beautiful boutique hotel in the middle of a hip neighborhood in downtown Miami, and any fear was replaced by fascination and awe.

I was out of Arizona and feeling free. Young rebellion, capitalist greed, desire for autonomy, illusions of fame and grandeur, were all factors in the push to want to "make it" in porn. But after my first scene, where we played all these fun college pranks and were laughing nonstop and found ourselves that night sitting by the beach eating steak listening to the waves of the ocean with money in our pockets, I thought to myself, "Maybe this life would be nice." My pause for reflection about if this career choice would damage my reputation long term or make life harder in the future went like this:

Me: If I decide to do this it could impact my future.

Me: Yeah, but the world is evolving, and people are more open minded.

Me: That's true. Plus, I'm definitely going to be successful. I'm not, like, dumb.

Me: True. But what about a future partner/ husband?

Me: Any man that loves me will love me regardless.

Me: What do you think your family will think?

Me: My dad will hate it. But I know him and mom love me unconditionally.

Me: Maybe I'll change porn. Maybe I can be different, more authentic.

Me: Start my own production company?

Me: That's actually hot real sex? Yes!!

Me: Ok, so it's decided. I'm going for it, to the best of my abilities, I will be successful.

When I came back from Miami I was flying high with possibilities, but that was quickly shattered with a knock on the door. Nyx opened it and was handed a service notice. She got served. Well, I got served but we were two almost identical young women with blonde hair, it didn't matter. I was the recipient of a $50,000 lawsuit from the non-nude solo girl website. They told me when we first started that if I decided to not work with them anymore, they would keep the content they produced of me and continue to sell and make money off it, and I thought that's exactly what they would do. But because I had done porn they were pissed off, who would want solo-girl or tease style content when they could see me get railed by a hot young dude on a tube site? The lawsuit was for the amount of money they *could* have made on me over the course of however many days/years.

The thing about lawsuits is even if they are contractually bogus, once they've begun you have to follow a certain procedure to fight them, or they win by default. Somehow, I was able to keep them at bay for months while I figured out how to fight them and come up with my master plan for taking over porn. Lily LeBeau, spelled with an e, was born in Miami, but she wasn't fully formed or conceptualized yet. My own sexuality at that time, barely explored.

I then proceeded to jump headfirst into the shark tank of the adult film industry. The beginning was a little rocky. The random stranger online aka "suitcase pimp" who had gotten me the job in Miami had another job for me in Los Angeles and flew me out there, and upon my arrival proceeded to convince me to film a "scene" with him. He had loaned me some money, $300, so I could go shopping at the mall. In exchange I'd shoot this scene with him later.

At the hotel that afternoon, smelling like my newly bought bottle of Euphoria by Calvin Klein, I watched as he attempted to do the scene. He bumbled around with his tripod, camera on top and still plugged into the wall because he forgot to charge it. He acted super nervous and awkward, and when it was finally time to have sex, he couldn't achieve an erection. He was wearing a condom even though he had shown me an industry approved STD test before we started.

About halfway through this sad act, I realized what was going on. That he just wanted to fuck, or at least try to cheaply live his dream of cosplaying porn star with a naive prospect. Watching his limp dick flop around in that condom gave me some sick pleasure. Oh, sweet budding sadism.

I wasn't happy, but I wasn't traumatized either, because at the time I had no reservations about what I was doing. I was ignorantly blissful and in my mind the job was to get paid to have sex on camera. I just felt like this was another job and I was more turned off and annoyed by how pathetic and sad it all became, the feeling of being tricked. But the *pleasure* I felt when he was looking so stressed and embarrassed with his flaccid dick in his hands trying to beat the life into it and failing, was honestly payment enough. Yes, he had duped me in a sense, he wasn't a legit producer he was just some random dude, and his karma came swiftly, though he did not. And I got to see it.

As luck would have it the next day on set, I was informed by the director that this man was indeed a suitcase-pimp. We call them that because they are not licensed and bonded in the state of CA which costs like $10,000. That was a life changing day and also may I add, an iconic scene. An 18-year-old girl from Payson, Arizona skating through Venice Beach, California, dressed like a slut, having the time of her life with strange old men. At the time the only thing I was scared of was those roller skates. The scene that day ended up being super hot, and I have fans still talking about it decades later. It's wild how these passing moments just become immortalized in your brain and in the culture.

During the shoot that day the director had been talking to a legitimate porn agent and friend of his who could help me and ideally represent me. After my scene it felt as though he gently picked me up and placed me in the lap of a nice fuzzy wolf who said all the right things, put me in a new hotel and promised me the world. What big hair you have! The better to keep my secrets with! What big eyes you have! The better to see how to manipulate you! What big teeth you have! The better to… well you'll find out.

The thrill was amazing, feeling like a bad girl who gets naked in front of horny old men and has sex with strangers. Yet, there was also a sense of comfort and belonging. They loved me, they were funny and gave me compliments, I was booked quickly and started to bring in some cash. At no point did I ever sexually desire the majority of these men, but feeling desired was the game each of us was playing, both receiving benefit if only to our ego. Remember, the job is sex, so you want to feel as sexy as possible, and you want to make the other person feel sexy and desired as well. The better performers can do that the hotter the scene will be and sometimes you roleplay so hard you actually cum!

Another part of the job of a new performer is to be taken on "Go Sees" by the agency, kinda like in NY, except you get naked. They would drive you all around the San Fernando Valley and you would go to each of the major production offices. The protocol was to go in, say hi, take your clothes off, spin in a circle, then they would ask you, usually while you were still naked, "So, do you like sex?"

This is part of the grooming process. Or, an "introduction to the culture" is probably a nicer way to say it. Things were way different in the early 2000s, and it was still a predator's playground, though most played by the rules. While I have my own experience, and I believe in the freedom of speech and I'm against censorship, I refuse to lie and say everyone was a safe fluffy teddy bear. Imagine being honest when they asked you questions? Ok I have, and this is what I think it would look like:

Director: Oh, look at you! How old are you?

Me: 18 (smiles innocently)

Director: So, do you like sex?

Me: Well, I've only had sex with like a few other people before this, so I have no clue really what sexuality is. But that's what makes me easily moldable and complacent. As well as genuinely excited to do anything beyond what is asked to prove that I belong here!

Director: Exactly what we're looking for.

Me: Thank you for confirming my worth!

Director: Ok, take off your clothes and let's see that body!

Me: No problem. I'm very self-conscious of my body since modeling and have been doing a lot of drugs lately at raves so I'm pretty skinny and hoping that pleases you.

Director: It does!!

Me: YAY!

Assistant: You're doing great, honey.

Me: (beams with a false sense of confidence)

And that was it. Almost immediately I was living, breathing, and hardcore fucking the fantasy! In my head I was a bad-ass and rebel, and I adored all my misfit coworkers and irreverent days on set with the different studios. I was thrilled with the constantly changing, exciting, shiny life that was magically appearing in front of me. Life was a movie! On location in Malibu watching the sunset, or spending days in mansions, warehouses, different sets and studios all spread out throughout the San Fernando Valley and Los Angeles, each bringing with it a particular brand of insanity and fun.

Big giant personalities, both in the directors and the talent. Life was never dull. The different scenes and the sex was just the backdrop, in front of me was adulthood, womanhood, finally living life on my terms. I was making my way in the world and about 6 months into my new career. So of course, I went for the 3- bedroom with vaulted ceilings in the heart of Porn Valley, Woodland Hills, California! This was it, I was going to be successful so, why not go big?

Up until then I had been making the trip back and forth with my friend Nyx from Phoenix. We would drive the 6 hours in my Chevy Blazer, stay for two weeks in a cheap hotel, go to a few raves and techno parties and then come home. This was also the time my mom found out. She was always nosey and persistent with her communication. She knew something was up when I was avoiding her calls and visits. Sorry, Mom! I'm in LA making porn.

Everyone wants to know what my parents think about my career. My mom accepted my choices, and it did not fracture our relationship, though it worried her deeply the stigma she knew I would face. Her biggest concern has always been to know that I'm safe, so though she did not agree with my choice, she never cut off communication with me. We'll get to my dad later.

Things had been steadily improving and I was working consistently. The new agency was working out. Taking the plunge and getting an apartment in Woodland Hills was the commitment needed to send me to the next level. Living in the heart of porn valley, ready to work, I was (mostly) dependable and delivered a good scene, and might I add, a delight to have on set. I started gaining traction and caught the attention of a Japanese production company when they were filming in LA. When asked if I would go to Japan for 7 days to shoot porn my answer was an enthusiastic yes! That was one of the best experiences of my life.

Another popular porn star and me were both flown out to Tokyo, Japan and stayed in an adorable tiny hotel in the city. The days we spent working were full of unusual sex acts, like being covered head to toe in seaweed jelly (that was the other girl) or dressing as a cosplay character with body armor and a sword (that was me). The male actors were hidden away, and we only met them minutes before the scene started. They were so respectful. I had to convince one to be a little rough with me, I thought he was so sexy and wanted to push him to get a little freakier. I wish I knew the names of any of the male performers I worked with over there, but alas. Japan has a very different culture around sex work.

We did some sightseeing in between workdays and visited some temples and tourist spots. There is a famous restaurant called Ninja Bar, and I highly recommend it to anyone going to Tokyo. When you arrive, you have to go through a trap door (they have an alternative path for differently abled people). Inside felt straight out of a movie, and the ambiance at night was elegant and mysterious Plus, the magic tricks at the table added to mystique, and I found myself laughing all night.

Our host loved to drink and at that time so did I! Though I was disappointed to discover the legal drinking age in Japan was 20 because during that trip I turned 19 and was sure that I'd be able to partake legally. Still, I managed to have a good time. And the other girl even smuggled weed over in her vibrator! In hindsight this was probably really dumb, but we rolled joints and smoked out the tiny balcony of our hotel and then wandered the city taking it all in.

Everything was different and exciting, the vending machines, the 7/11s, but the memory that sticks out the most in my mind was the day spa we went to! There had to be 20 different baths, some filled with water with silk, some a certain temperature or enriched with a specific mineral. The coed part was like a little village with heated floors and food and ice cream and anything you could want, simply charged to your wrist band. The outdoor area was my favorite, with the individual wooden hot tubs sitting beneath the climbing vines and flowers on the ceiling. Looking up, I felt so fucking blessed. Best spa experience of my life to date.

When I returned from Japan in January of 2010 things were on a roll, Nyx had been staying with me more frequently, and Twitter had just become a thing. Nyx was looking to be represented by the best of the best, and the best was Mark Spiegler. He'd represented just about all the women we idolized before getting into the industry. I was still working with my first agency and living in my expensive three-bedroom apartment with vaulted ceilings and next to no furniture.

I was booking some work but not to the extent I needed to be able to afford my bills and lifestyle, buy clothing for shoots, and pay for the monthly mandatory STI testing. I found a temporary roommate on set one day in the form of a British guy who used to be in some boy band in the UK back in the 80s, and was now a middle-aged drunk who knew all the coolest bars in Downtown Hollywood. I don't remember the names, but I remember the red velvet interior and the rich history embedded in every crack and corner and wall.

He didn't last long as my roommate because his persistence in wanting to fuck me became really annoying. I did let him lick my pussy one night mostly out of pity and exhaustion, but we never fucked. He started painting really dark pictures in his empty bedroom and his moodiness and depression became a constant subject. I had to ask him to leave.

After him I had another female performer move in with me and that helped a bit, but she had her own emotional instability and life challenges and while she never directed them at me her life was hard, and it stressed her out and caused her to not be able to work often. Stability for both of us seemed a long way away.

Because of this constant stress in my home and finances and lack of coping skills, I was still self-harming but trying hard not to because cuts and scrapes and bruises show up on camera. It's a lot harder to hide these things when you are required to be naked for your job. During this time period I also met a famous French DJ at some electronic party. Nyx was a fan and ended up getting us backstage. Him and I began a long-distance friendship which eventually became romantic.

My financial situation became desperate after some time and the fault was almost entirely my own. When I signed my contract with the wolf, remember those big teeth? They told me that if at any point I wanted out of this 2-year contract that it's not a problem just to let them know. So that's what I did.

Stupid, stupid girl.

Suddenly, my work was drying up, they knew I had a fancy new apartment to pay for, so I was being offered a 6 guy blowbang for $600 (way under-rate) and then told that I could buy myself out of my contract for $600. My pride was too strong, that would be the only money I would potentially get to pay my now past due rent and they were going to take it. And a scene like that would normally pay at least $1000 and since I'd never done a blow bang it would be considered a "first" and I could ask even more money for it. They knew all this. They were devouring me!!

So, I found a lawyer. He had interest in this case because as he explained to me this is a tactic not so great agencies use to keep talent but it's illegal to force someone to have sex for their work. So, if they pursued this contract in court and I won, it would set a "precedent" so that agencies would not be able to do this anymore. Somehow the angels were listening and Mark Spiegler found out about this. He thought what they were doing was shitty and he helped me get a few scenes under the table so I could pay my rent and get my bills caught up and even said he would represent me, but I had to drop the lawsuit.

I became a Spiegler girl in the spring of 2010 and not working was a thing of the past. He really is the best of the best and he knows how to get his girls work. He's smart, charismatic, and teaches you like a really temperamental and sometimes grumpy dad who's not above ripping you a new one when you mess up or don't follow the rules. Which were: always answer your phone, don't make me look bad, and don't be late. He's irreverent and makes horrible jokes and loves watching old movies, and he turned me into a professional porn star. I found community as a Spiegler girl and was given 24 crazy sexy sisters. It was an unspoken requirement that we get along and not act like catty bitches. We tried our best and mostly succeeded. There was a lot of love and support between all us girls, it was somewhat opposite of my days in NY.

Every girl has a different body type and niche so even though we are somewhat competing for jobs there is plenty of work to go around. There's big booty girls, gonzo girls, the acting and big movie features girls, high dollar, lower dollar, black, white, Latina, foreign... The list goes on. There were plenty of niches to go around.

Spiegler knew how to keep us all hungry for success yet also satisfied with more work than we could ask for. There was no saying no to scenes. If a company wanted you, you were booked. When you were just starting out there was no being picky about male actors. You showed up and delivered an award-winning scene every time, no matter what. That's what was expected of Spiegler girls, and the return is the highest respect in the industry. We may do some of the most intense hardcore scenes in the biz, but no one fucks with us or our money, because no one fucks with Spiegler.

We knew it and all the directors knew it, though some still tried to push boundaries, they were faced with the wrath of Spiegs, and trust me, nobody wants that. But within that circle of protection there was still the knowing that we were part of a greater porn industry with its own politics and culture.

There is propaganda in our industry as any other. Things we avoid talking about and things we may overly glorify. It's all part of the fantasy, and more importantly the PR. We handle our business internally, don't talk to the press, they always misrepresent us, we don't need more bad publicity so don't talk about our sob stories or feed into the cliche we all come from broken beginnings. Stuff like that.

With the rise of my success was also the rise of my problems with my vagina. Sorry if that's gross but it's the truth. I learned quickly this was an industry based on one's physical health and ability to do the job. As someone who's had cold sores since teenagerhood I knew that when I became exhausted, I would have an outbreak, but this job was testing me on a whole different level.

A yeast infection while filming a porno? With a black performer? BV during a girl-on-girl scene? Literally a circle of hell. Without sharing the details just know, especially those first few years, I experienced every single circle of hell you can imagine. Both being the one causing the hell, and the one receiving it. Mostly you try to be compassionate, to yourself and others. We know the job. And bodies will be bodies, but sometimes it felt like my body had a personal vendetta against me, protesting at the worst possible and least expected moments.

Sometimes I would be working so much that when the rare occurrence of chlamydia or gonorrhea would pop up, I took it as a welcomed forced vacation. Obviously, you can't work, and it's not technically your fault so no one can really be mad, and you have a mandatory window from antibiotics until next test that you have to wait and you can't be fucking at that time. It was glorious. My pussy got a break, and I could live life for a little bit.

Those occurrences were not as common as the mainstream would like to believe. I've gotten Chlamydia twice and Gonorrhea twice. And half of those cases have been from fucking a person outside of the industry. That number still stands and I'm going on 20 years of being sexually active, my body count in the hundreds. I'd like to mention though, because we are tested about every 14 days, while working in the industry I've never had an infection for longer than that. The quicker you find out and treat an STI the less damage it can cause to your body. I wish more people out in the real world were better at getting tested regularly. If we just had a national STD testing day once a month, we could basically knock out some of the most common STDs. But everyone would have to do it, and for some reason even getting tested brings feelings of shame and fear for a lot of people.

By the Summer of 2010 I really started to feel at home in LA. I downsized to a 2-bedroom apartment in the same complex and had a new roomie who was perfect for me, Sarah Shevon. We were both into healthy eating, she had a cute cat named Kitty, was proficient at spinning vinyl on her decks, and brought and installed her own stripper pole, plus she loved smoking weed as much as me. We were both represented by Mark Spiegler and could lean on each other and relate to each other's journeys.

Sarah was also older than me and helped me to be a cleaner and more organized person. I was very bad at dishes when we lived together and hadn't mastered buying groceries for a single person so would often have food rot and go to waste. I know, I cringe thinking of that too. She was a good friend and had a big impact on my wellbeing and security during the time we lived together and helped me grow as an adult.

She is still battling Crohn's disease and Ulcerative Colitis and has an ongoing GoFundMe and if you want to donate, I have a link on the back page of this book.

There were industry parties quite often for different events and on the Fourth of July 2010, I would meet one of my dearest friends. Though she spoke no English and had recently arrived from France, Spiegler knew we would be good friends. He had a knack for pairing us girls up. Margot had dark brown wavy hair that came to just above her nipples and the most beautiful, tanned skin being of Tunisian and French ancestry. She was 5'4" and weighed 100lbs wet, was full of joie de vivre and a passion for living life, and though no one at that pool party knew what she was saying the guys and girls were falling in love with her left and right and she was having the time of her life kissing all of them. Though it was her first time in America, in France known by her stage name, Lou Charmelle, she was experiencing a rapid rise to fame. Margot was happy to be there and completely soaking up the lifestyle and anyone with eyes could see it, especially me.

Spiegler was right, I loved her immediately.

Margot was also into electronic music and became fast friends with Nyx, they could speak the same language in music, which I've never been really good at. They also matched each other's levels of exhibitionism and loved playing with the lines of being a slut and sexually empowered woman. I watched in awe, their biggest cheerleader, as I had not fully mastered this level of freedom IRL and enjoyed living vicariously through them. I preferred the safety and boundaries of expressing this side of myself on set, real life was way too complicated to navigate. Dodging men's sexual advances constantly was too much for me.

Easier to say no to them all and just be a whore on camera.

Besides, I've always been more of a love addict than a sex addict.

I was still talking to my famous DJ and things were getting more and more lovey-dovey. He was scheduled to film a music video with another French artist, and I thought that it would be cool to introduce him to Margot so they could speak French together. When I saw her again, I communicated this to her and surprisingly, she had a French rapper friend coming to LA to film a music video too and invited me to hang out! It took us some time to realize the two musicians were filming a music video together and we hadn't realized it. We both had famous French lovers, and our famous French lovers were filming a music video together in LA!

Talk about coincidence and a crazy night out. On the day of the music video, Nyx and I met our famous French DJ on Venice beach. We had a penchant for taking psychedelics on our days off and today we had some tasty acid on hand. Without much hesitation we each placed a tab on our tongues and teasingly offered some to our DJ friend. He accepted and would spend the entirety of that filming that day tripping balls on acid which is really funny to me when I watch the video now. At some point we got bored hanging around the set, we were not being paid to be there and went off adventuring. Nyx and I never had a hard time having fun, especially when high on acid.

When we returned hours later the crew, and some extras from the music video would go out for a night on Sunset Boulevard. Margot had finally joined us and with the 3 of us girls together, trouble was inevitable. The good kind. Sort of. The first thing I did was head to the bar and order a long island iced tea, because I'm fun when I'm drunk so of course I wanna make it happen fast. Unfortunately, I was also anorexic from the drugs and that was the last thing I remember until I came to naked in a jacuzzi with 3 other people, no fucking clue who they were. I was informed the next day I fucked the tour manager of the famous rapper.

The night turned into morning and the randos were kicked out and I finally got to be with my DJ! Of course, we fucked and of course it was super weird cause there was still a little acid floating in my system. Have you ever had sex on psychedelics? I'd like to try to have sex on acid again with someone I deeply love and see if the experience is more other worldly than *fucking weird as hell.* Still, I thought this meant he and I were progressing our long-distance texting relationship to the physical and I was so happy. At some point in the night, I had lost most of my clothes and he gave me his T-Shirt to go home in. It smelled sweaty like pine trees, and it was the most intoxicating scent I had ever smelled.

Blacking out that night was actually a terrifying experience for me. Remember when I said that Nyx and Margot matched each other's exhibitionism? Me in my right mind would not have fucked the tour manager, a bunch of randos from the bar, and the guy I was interested in dating, all on the same night. STDs actually do freak me out, and shitty sex is the bane of my existence. I'd rather have no sex than shitty sex, and in my opinion drunk sex is shitty sex. Fight me, I'm standing by it.

Unless I find an actual mental or emotional attraction to someone, they don't really turn me on. *What about all the guys you fuck on set?* There is a mental attraction there, there's a level of understanding and excitement in discovering how well we can perform together, they do excite me, but in a different way, more psychological than physical.

Still, when I'm smashed, I can be a huge lush and want to make out with everyone. Not the best when your prefrontal cortex is shut off and you're not actually in control of your body. And are navigating life as a totally hot babe. It's ok you don't have to feel sorry for me.

Me and my famous DJ's texting affair had been going on since before I met Spiegler and while I was dealing with my old agency's bullshit there was a time I had no money and my tabs were expired on my car and I was so desperate to see him I took the train from LA to San Francisco. It was a terrible idea and in my diary, I wrote,

He said if you still come you're either crazy or madly in love. To which I thought, well I don't feel sanely in love.

Bitch, no. It was peak groupie behavior, but I thought I was becoming more to him than that. Oh, the naivety of 19. After San Francisco and seeing each other in LA for his music video, I wanted time with him all to myself so we planned a visit for me to come to France for a week.

And what an overwhelmingly wonderful first trip out of the US by myself that was! My first time in Paris, with a guy who was successful in his career as I was finally building more and more success in mine. He was telling me he loved me (first) and that he couldn't wait for the people on his street to talk about his American girlfriend Lacy, and for me to speak French.

The dream was so good and I thought because of my work that I understood him and his lifestyle and even though he was 35 with an ex-baby mama and 5 year old child and a weirdly close relationship with his "best girl friend" it wasn't a big deal because I'm such a cool girl, even after I walked out on him and that best girl friend kissing one night when we all went out to the bar, I kept my composure. Because then his gay best friend kissed him, so it was funny and we all laughed!

No one kissed me.

The red flags were there. The chain smoking, the weird groupies that hung around, the clear and proud self-hatred, the nearly overdosing on MDMA because he "just wanted to feel happy". But who was I to judge? One of his friends was making fun of me one night and drinking out of a baby bottle that was in the kitchen, mocking me for being young and I just thought, you look like a fucking idiot. But that was one of his friends. So I laughed and pretended like I didn't understand French as she gulped water out of a plastic nipple while everyone laughed.

Another one of the girls who had a crush on the DJ befriended me and promised me that nothing was happening between her and him. He talked about her like she was a crazy obsessive psycho, yet invited her to everything. It was weird but I didn't care. Disfunction was fine with me, as long as I had him. That week passed so fast, and he took me to all the most magical spots. One night we went to the lookout deck of the Eiffel Tower while it was raining, and I had this moment where I felt my aunt's spirit. She always loved to travel and loved Paris. Because it was raining, I just allowed myself to cry and it felt so good. I felt like she was so proud of me for getting out and seeing the world. The last night I was with him we watched movies until my taxi came at 4am. We watched *The Car Keys*, (*Les Clés de Bagnole*), a French absurd film which I enjoyed a lot! And *The Hate* (*La Heine*), about police brutality in Paris in the 90s. I told him I could come for a month next time. Do some work in Budapest and make some money out here. One week just wasn't enough. We were in love, and I would find a way to make it work. Plus spending more time in Paris didn't sound too bad! He seemed happy about the idea.

Upon my arrival on my 2nd visit a few months later things were different. There was drama with his ex-baby mama. Somehow, she had been violently attacked by a gang in the street and needed him to take care of her. So after only a few days at his apartment he asked if I could stay somewhere else. How could I say no? What a terrible misfortune! That's literally crazy. I quickly got a few things together and found a hostel nearby, took only what I needed and left, forgetting my smartphone behind. Luckily, I had a tiny EU flip phone.

At the hostel there was a lovely Spanish man who worked behind the counter who I chatted with when I arrived. I settled into my room and then decided to wander around the city a bit. Everything was still so new and exciting, just walking around was an experience. I found myself at a cute typical Parisian bar and sat down to have a mojito. The bartender was a middle-aged French guy and he kept supplying me mojitos. The language barrier prevented deep conversation, but he kept making me drinks, on the house, and promised me something to eat. A free meal? When I'm now having to pay $30 a night to stay at a hostel when I thought I was going to be staying for free with my boyfriend? Give it to me, Monsieur. But le Monsieur was smart, and he took his sweet ass time with the food. He was getting ready to close up by the time the fucking french fries showed up. French fries? I thought I was getting a meal here Mr. Restaurant owner? No, the drinks were on the house for a reason. Now, after midnight and seemingly without a better option I hopped on the back of his moped and he took me to my hostel. At the doorway he asked if he should get a room here. I said, no, goodnight, but somehow, he couldn't understand. There was a scuffle at the door of me trying to go inside while keeping him out and to my delight the lovely Spanish guy caught on to what was happening and stepped in. Sorry Monsieur, the hostel is for guests only.

The Spanish guy from the front desk, Marco, and I cracked open a few cervezas and started telling each other about our lives. He lived on an artist commune 40 minutes outside of the city and I was the unhoused wanna-be girlfriend of a famous French DJ. When my initial stay at the hostel was complete, Marco offered to let me stay at his place for a few days until I was scheduled to leave for Budapest for work. I accepted and as I sat on the train taking me out of the familiar tall yet known architectural giants of the city into the more open and more unknown French countryside I wondered if this was a good idea.

When I arrived, Marco explained to me that the artist commune was actually a well-organized squat, it's a whole thing in France, squatters taking over places, there's even festivals and meetups around it. It's a grey area of legality in France. Marco's artistic contribution to the artist's squat was musical bicycles, bikes with tubes attached to the sides and a mechanism to make them play sound when ridden. It was pretty cool, and so was his flat. The whole squatter mentality is to build what you need yourself with material you have. And he had built an entire loft with a bathtub on the top level, his kitchen counter was an old door, and his home was a hodgepodge of plants, trinkets, and old furniture, and of course bikes. The entire front wall was made up of giant windows, some were broken, and that made it more beautiful and special to be there. At night we would buy rum, and his friends would come over and sing songs. Marco played the bass which was a bucket with a pole and string attached to it. His friends played the violin, accordion, and clarinet, and I felt like I was living in 1920's Paris. None of them tried to fuck me, and they were all so welcoming and kind. I felt really safe with them.

On my last night there, Marco and I watched *Mulholland Drive*, I guess because I live in LA and it's iconic but, holy Jesus. That was a weird movie. And when it was over Marco asked me if I wanted to fuck as we had been sleeping in the same bed together for days with no attempts on his or my part. It was weird timing after the movie. I kindly said no, and he told me that usually girls who sleep in his bed fuck him and seemed genuinely perplexed but totally accepting of me not wanting to.

Soon I was flying to Budapest, full of confidence in my desire to work in Europe even though everyone had warned me the prices are way lower. They were high enough to pay for the rest of my trip and that was my only goal at that moment. Budapest is beautiful. I like going to places for work because you have someone who is helping you. My European agency's driver picked me up from the airport and brought me to the model apartment while showing me some of the sights on the way.

It was fall and the leaves were changing. The dark gothic architecture and old trees make Budapest a gorgeous place to be in the fall. Cold, but pretty. The blessings of being in work mode were that I had many things to do and buy before I could start shooting. First check in to the model apartment, then go to the testing center to get tested. Then figure out how to get to the mall to buy some shoot clothes, and on the way home go to the grocery store to buy any food or toiletries I may need.

Going to foreign grocery stores are one of my favorite fucking things in this world and I can browse them for hours. It's so fun and exciting to see the different flavors and treats and the smells! Ever since Panama, I go crazy for the slightly mildewy humid cleaning product smell that most bodega and low budget grocery stores smell like. I am obsessed with that smell! It has to have some of the mildew along with the cleaning product smell and I guess the humidity is just a natural byproduct of that. Anyway, I'm getting off topic.

Being on set in Europe had all the same makings of back home. There was paperwork, there was make-up, there were photos, sex stills, and video and of course money. However, the attitudes were different, colder, more cynical and business-like. Not rude, but blunt, less joyful. That seems like an Eastern European thing, there are not as many giggles over there. The girls I worked with were great, some didn't even speak English, but everyone did the job and went home with a paycheck. I was booked solid for almost 12 days straight. It was really challenging keeping up with the different early call times and late nights on set and towards the end of the trip I was completely fucking exhausted.

I took the night train back to Paris from Budapest and woke up in the German countryside in the morning light, as well as what seemed to be 3 cold sores forming on my lip. It made sense, I was in full starvation mode, food had lost its priority after day 3, while barely sleeping and being on set for 6-10 hours a day… of course my body was pissed. Throughout the hostel, the squat, Budapest, and then coming back to Paris I had been communicating with my famous DJ boyfriend on my piece of crap flip phone, the kind where you have to press the number multiple times to write 1 letter, and things were wild with his ex-baby mama. She was suicidal and having a complete mental breakdown from the attack, so I was only able to go into his place on the last morning of my trip to get my stuff that had been left there. We didn't talk, he was like the shadow on the wall after an atomic bomb, remnants of what used to be a person. A person who had a month ago told me he couldn't wait until I spoke French and for the neighbors to know all about this American now living in Paris. He couldn't even speak to me now.

When I walked inside there were boxes of bandages on the table and some other first aid kit items, but in my gut, everything felt so off. It looked set up, most of it hardly used. None of it made sense but I couldn't question anything because of how serious the situation was. What an asshole that would make me! He was leaving for a gig later that day and offered to share a taxi with me to the airport. How nice of him.

After I had gathered my suitcases, and met him downstairs at the taxi, this was the first time I had seen him in almost a month. I sat there feeling so defeated, so ugly with my massive herpes outbreak on my upper lip, and the realization that whatever I thought this was, was no more. During the taxi ride, him, his manager, and I sat in heavy silence. At the airport I tried to feign a smile with the 3 cold sores taking up all the real estate on my face. I was so ashamed and embarrassed but still holding on to hope, any hope, I could manage.

He would go on to fuck the girl he said was obsessive, she would get a tattoo for him, and then he would marry the best girl friend. I think they have a kid together now. He is a pathological liar. I remained friends with a few people I met when I was in France and years later would have a mutual friend tell me that indeed, it was all a lie, the attack, the baby mama's suicidality, everything a lie because he couldn't just tell me he didn't want me to stay at his apartment. All the people around him could see what he was doing to me but do nothing about it. They worked for him or his label or wanted to work with him creatively, I was just some 19-year-old American porn whore with stars in her eyes. The mutual friend felt bad, and I guess him telling me the truth was his way of giving me closure and validation for what I went through. And yeah, I did act like a lovesick puppy and go to the ends of the earth to see him, but I thought we were in love, he said he loved me, I felt so lucky to be that girl. He wanted me to meet his father while I was in Paris. He loved to feed the fantasy. He was as old then as I am now. 35.

The final thing he said to me is that if I needed to understand, I could watch *The Last Tango in Paris*. It would be years before I had the courage to, and thank God I fucking waited. It's a French movie about an older man who falls for a much younger woman and they have an anonymous sexual affair, she wants him but he doesn't want her, he rapes her, then decides he wants her suddenly but she no longer wants him, and when he comes to her begging for her to take him back she takes a gun and shoots and kills the guy.

Seriously??? Ugh. Men.

He was fucking toxic, and it messed with my head. On the bright side, that deep devastating pain opened a well of delicious juicy melancholic creativity. I've always loved writing songs and lyrics and while I was yearning to be with him but sensing in my soul it was the end, all I could do was write song after song while sitting in various Paris cafes with rain and historic buildings as my backdrop and muse. Sadness is my path to creativity and though it hurt so very much at the time, the experience of being in Paris and Budapest and meeting people there was just the beginning of my European love affair. He left a mark on my soul, but more importantly, so did the desire to see and experience as much as I possibly could of Europe.

***

My heart was in pieces, but the blow was softened because I had made pretty good money in Budapest. Which I then proceeded to hand all $7500 over to those fucking bastards with the non-nude solo girl website's $50,000 lawsuit so we could "settle out of court." Yeah, you forgot about that didn't ya? Not even a year had passed since I was served. Wild, right?

My lawyer friend told me this was the best way to make this finally go away and I agreed. I was glad I had the money when the moment came. It had worked out well for me timing wise because during my visit to Europe the porn industry shut down in the US because someone had tested positive for HIV. They stopped shooting for something like 2 weeks, but it didn't affect Europe. Things tend to work out for me, even when they don't.

***

Back home in porn valley circa 2010/2011 I was making my way as a Spiegler girl and had even garnered some nominations at the awards show the following January. Best new Starlet, and a handful of others. People ask me about my favorite scenes, but I barely remember a quarter of them. Life was a blur-fast forwarding in front of me. Years passed like seconds, traumas, scandals and change came and went. It's hard to connect all the dots. What happened when and in what order, with time things bleed into each other. I was becoming a successful and now internationally known porn star, but I couldn't tell at that time. My focus was on earning my place with the best of the best performers and I had begun thinking about how I would like to start my own production company.

During awards season, I didn't win best new starlet, or any awards that year, but I truly embodied the porn spirit. I had the hottest date, a well-known fetish producer, I was feeling on fire with all my outfits, and there is a notorious clip of me flashing my tits at the camera at the AVN award show. I was also intoxicated most of the time, but I'm a fun drunk and it's a fucking porn convention. This was appropriate behavior, and no one cared as long as I didn't make a fool of myself or overdose.

At the after party, I wound up hanging with some of the kinkier people from the industry and soon I was getting my face slapped and my butt spanked by one of the hottest dommes in the biz while people smoked a joint in a circle around us, fully clothed watching the spectacle. Doug Benson was just sitting there, smoking. They passed the joint around the circle, and this mega babe went to town slapping my face, telling everyone how much I liked it. Oh no, I loved it. Though, I might have scared Doug Benson.

I'd been making my mark as a bit of a masochist, surprise surprise. It was a healthy outlet for intense sensation and participating in these violent acts at this age felt very "bad kid", but not "self-harming emo." Taking control of my body by saying yeah, I can push you to certain limits and it's ok, and exploring these intense sensory experiences with others who are trained to do so safely is also totally fine. Bruises are fine. Getting slapped, spanked, and destroyed is fine. It's a full-on mind-body journey with another human, sometimes multiple humans. I feel thankful that I felt safe enough to do so many crazy things on and off camera with the Kink community. This little AVN spectacle was nothing.

I'd been working a lot at kink.com. I felt like I fit in with the kink people. Intellectuals, usually falling somewhere on the neurodivergent spectrum, open minded, vibrant, genuine people who fight for things they believe in. They have strong voices, and strong opinions, and I liked how structured and consistent the kink world was. You knew what to expect because there were a clear set of rules that everyone follows. But even within that safety and structure, I wasn't totally sure that I fit. I didn't have anything I was fighting for, I wasn't an activist. And I didn't know all the correct inclusive words to say, but I listened and tried to learn and they seemed to love me nonetheless, and I love the kink community.

The porn star archetype idolizes a certain type of performance, highly sexual, thinks like a guy as in is always horny and ready for sex at the drop of a hat, loves everything about sex, and never fakes an orgasm. The kink ideal is slightly different, it's who has the most open mind, who has explored the deepest darkest parts of sexuality, who can expand further and be more creative than the other, and return from these depths with wisdom, strength, surety of self, not insanity. Kink world felt more authentic to me because even if it was still a fantasy, it came from a more real place.

I still struggled with identity. It felt like I was playing a game of chicken, like who's going to drop the act first and be like, just kidding. I know we're all perverts but sometimes my head spins with what's for clout and what's real. How much are we all performing and how much is genuine? And can any of us even tell anymore?

It's so hard to know and I think a lot of people don't drop the act. It's not an act, it's a lifestyle. It's a culture. It's a society. I genuinely believe that for many of us it's an identity. *Slut* means so much more than someone who is sexually active. It's a slur, it's a badge, it's a weapon, it's liberation, it's blasphemy. *Slut* is our ancestral shame and the medicine to that shame. Maybe we all get lost in our own characters and delusions of grandeur sometimes, maybe that's ok. Our job is to perform and to entertain. Some people are method actors.

I happen to bond with the more musical and creative types rather than the sexually deviant types. Don't get me wrong I love my industry but outside of it I'm just, Lacy. Sensitive artists, deep thinking creatives, the musically guided, those tend to be who I resonate with the most. I can't be a bimbo, or full time kinkster, I don't have any daily fetish needs, but I do need to be able to be understood as an artist and sensitive soul. Porn will destroy someone who is too sensitive. I'm always finding some new way to express myself creatively and I'm a sucker for anyone who meets me on this level.

That's how he got me, Angel. Well, the first time he didn't actually get me. We worked together on set, and he gave me his number, and I lost it when I got a new phone. I was so bummed because I had no way to get a hold of him. We were soon scheduled to shoot together again, and I would spend all day on set making out with him between takes. The makeup artist was annoyed by our unprofessional behavior and constantly having to retouch my makeup, but the connection between us was electrifying. He sealed the deal while I was smoking a cigarette outside. I wanted to record some songs (the sad ones I wrote in Paris), and he knew how to use music software because he was in a synthcore metal band.

Perfect excuse to see each other again.

We found all the excuses to see each other, and he would make the drive from downtown LA to Woodland Hills weekly just to spend the evenings with me. As two working professionals we kept independently busy and when we were together it was so nice to be able to talk to someone who knew, who got it, who could complain about the same directors keeping you on set for 16 hour days, or laugh about the fact Spiegler kept making fun of him for being gay because he did gay porn a few times. It was all so stupid and being with him felt like being able to stand apart from the things that were unimportant like porn politics and bullying behavior and focus on what was important. Our little creative projects.

The gears were still turning in my head conceptualizing having my own production company, making my own movies. OnlyFans did not exist at this time. At that time the options were to sign with a platform of sites, similar to what those guys were doing with my solo girl site, the tech and developers, not amateur porn producers, having all the power because they had the knowledge and skills to manage and run the site, or you could get a word press site and try to do it yourself. I've never been a tech girl.

The internet came out when I was a teenager and I had Myspace and a flip phone, but I never graduated past the pre-made templates phase. I knew I had to have content to launch with, so I focused on that while I looked into the mainstream world to help me build and manage my site.

Angel was a film graduate from UCLA and loved the filmmaking process. He was a huge help in filming and editing many of the videos, and he was usually willing to lend his dick when we decided to film sexy videos ourselves. Life felt purposeful, it felt creative and collaborative. I was connecting with other performers and making friends shooting my own content and thinking about becoming a business owner at 20 years old.

I knew I'd be successful!

I'm not dumb like those other girls.

There were cracks beneath the surface. The cracks of my own psyche and traumas, still unresolved. The people pleasing and masking were also in full force. I was Lily LaBeau, a famous porn star living in Los Angeles, possessing the ability to bring grown men to their knees! Yet in my heart I wanted to make friends both inside and outside the adult industry, not scare or intimidate people. I'd become a novelty, even to those who'd known me before the industry, and I had to live up to their expectations now.

I tried my very best.

But making people uncomfortable became inherent with my job title. I'd say *porn star* and the switch was flipped, I was no longer human, I was an object of desire to be conquered or dissected. I was also still suffering from disordered eating, constant vaginal problems, relationship challenges, and a pervasive feeling that I don't belong, which just made me want to prove it more.

I am porn, I am a real pervert, I love sex, I am a sex goddess. Thankfully I was too delusional to see where the act ended, and I began. I was fully committed to the role. Plus, I was really happy with Angel and the life we had. We never fought, we were so sweet, so kind, so thoughtful, so supportive, the love he gave felt real and genuine and built off mutual interests. That first year, I thought he would be the man I would marry.

But I was 20 years old and still loved a good and wild adventure.

The best part about Angel and me was that we were not very co-dependent the first year. We'd go days without texting because we'd both be on set or working and there was no stress about that. We knew the others' values around work, we had our spoken boundaries around scenes, and we bonded over similar complaints of the industry so I was never scared he would be forced to do something potentially harmful or against his limits. Cheating wasn't a concern either because we didn't need to. I knew who he was fucking, and he knew who I was fucking, off set we were each other's only. That was the deal, and it worked.

Plus, I was living the dream! He was a part of it but definitely never the whole thing. We each had our own lives, passions, interests and friend groups which intersected at the porn world. I had my agency sisters and Spiegler was always so good at bringing us together, for the parties, the awards shows, various holidays, and even just hangouts at his apartment.

It felt like my own version of family.

In January during awards season, I was again nominated for AVN awards and in the middle of that week I would be turning 21! I was signing for a company at the awards show that year, meaning I got paid to go to the convention and stand there and sign photos for fans at my company's booth. It was great because you got paid per day and they covered the cost of the hotel. I loved it! I love meeting fans and getting dressed cute and scribbling my signature on all kinds of things! My favorite being the time I signed a guy's dick and then he came back the next day and showed me a video of him jerking off with my signature on his dick!

I reveled in the taboo! I loved the naughtiness and the acceptance of deviance! Anything goes. Sure, some people came to the convention who were actually bad people looking to do bad things and with bad intentions, but mostly, it was fans who just loved porn and were so happy and nervous to meet their favorite girls.

Margot would make another 3-month trip to the US and use my couch as homebase for the duration of it. We bonded even deeper with her newly acquired English language skills. She amazed me with the progress she made after mere months. She practiced on her own every day and voila! She and I could actually communicate. She was a firecracker! A bit crazy but never boring. A ball of energy with a vibrancy and zest for life I'd never seen. She seemed to have no shame, no reservations about anything.

I loved her. Even if she scared me a little.

We both loved traveling, and she had made friends through her porn work all over Europe and we had begun devising a 6-week European vacation together! She knew about everything that happened with the famous French DJ and she knew, together we could have an amazing and different experience. Europe was still calling to me and what better way to discover it than with my new best friend who knew all of the most amazing spots to go!

Spiegler was not happy about this. Time brings clarity and I believe he had been working hard to guide my career with the expectation that I would be an award winner, and a star really. He wanted me to stay in LA during the summer because it was the peak time for major feature movies which would be the ones to win awards.

And he was right.

I should have stayed. I should have committed to my career and listened to his advice. This is another top 5 moment I deeply regret and wish now that I had done differently. I didn't like being told what to do and I felt forced into it. I was testing the boundaries of my own autonomy, in life and with him. He was a very controlling agent but that is why he makes the best of the best. He made me into a professional. We, Spiegler girls, are all equally scared and reverent to him. He told Margot if we went on this trip together that she was not a good friend and it would be detrimental to my career. I was too young and blinded by my own ideas at that time to hear him, truly hear what he was communicating, and too codependent and loyal to not go on the trip with Margot.

He was just overreacting.

Right?

We went ahead planning the trip.

He dropped her from his agency.

That summer Margot and I would get our wish and depart for our 6-week European vacation! Switzerland, Ibiza, Monegros, Bayonne, Bordeaux, Budapest! I started by flying and meeting Margot in Switzerland for a few days and then went solo to Budapest to work. Angel would fly out and meet me in Budapest and Margot would join for the second part of the trip. I could tell Angel was out of his comfort zone, but he was handling it all in stride.

My two loves, Margot and Angel, were very different people. Angel was straight edge, though during this trip he drank a few beers and smoked a little weed which I found so novel and fun to experience with him. Margot's motto was, too much is never enough, we'd shared many nights of substance fueled laughing fits and I was caught in the middle, trying to appease both. Ultimately my bad girl raver side is the one that won. We were in Ibiza! Of course I wanted to take some molly.

We stayed in the old town with beige cobblestone steps and old stone churches and buildings. Ibiza is so beautiful and full of wild nature and magical hidden beaches, and drug addicts, lots and lots of drug addicts. Everyone is there to party and enjoy the hedonistic lifestyle of the island. It's not as scary as you might imagine, it's paradise and can offer anything you could possibly want.

Coming back to the apartment after a full night dancing into the A.M., the party continued with more drugs and comfy outfits and sunglasses to protect our overly dilated eyes from the daylight now pouring in. The night before we had filmed a scene with a famous DJ Margot was friends with for a scene in a porn movie we were filming out there, *Manhunt Ibiza*. This was our first attempt at producing our very own feature length movie. This spontaneity and me having no reservations about sucking a stranger's dick and having my boyfriend film it, made Angel uneasy.

I remember the look on his face that morning after, tears in his eyes as he told me that he loved me and the scene the night prior had really affected him, and I remember how horrible I felt because I was high as a fucking kite and though I wanted to be empathetic and reassure him, I was annoyed he chose right now to have this very serious talk. I know he didn't do drugs and couldn't understand my conflict of literally not being capable of being there for him at that moment.

The next part of the trip there was a giant elephant that we carried with us, no one ever acknowledging, we were the drug addicts and he was the Debbie Downer. We went to a 24-hour festival in Monegros and I tried to be a supportive girlfriend and not do any ecstasy with the rest of the group. Worst decision of my life. 24 hours on nothing but red bull and overpriced beers? While the rest of the group danced excitedly into the am, Angel and I chose to hobble to the car in the now blazing morning heat after nearly freezing all night. It took us over an hour to find it. Tired and bodies aching from dancing for so long we fell asleep in the car waiting for the others.

Finally, back in Switzerland and at the end of our trip we had one more event planned. A Swiss-style pool party, which was actually a very small temporary pool that had been erected in the city, surrounded by a wood deck where people could sunbathe and show off in a bikini. Angel did acid with us that day and I have an image embedded in my memory of him giggling while eating coconut bathed in sunlight with the happiest smile on his face. It felt rare to see him that at ease, that joyful and carefree. It's one of my favorite memories we made together because he was so happy. We, finally for a moment on that entire trip, felt truly peaceful. No work, no shooting demands, no guilt about drugs, just two people seeing the world in rainbow fractals and laughing at the absurdity of it all, together.

A big part of me was mad that I felt like I had to choose between him and Margot. I was still on the fence about the life I wanted to live. Angel was 5 years older than me, and we were two very different people. He graduated from high school at 16 in order to escape from his home life, he went to college, finished, and then started in porn. He loved being in control and I was chaos embodied, whether I wanted to be or not. Opposites attract but that trip highlighted just how different we were, and it was the beginning of the end of our relationship. Though we couldn't admit it yet.

After a year of dating Angel and I had decided to live together in Koreatown, Los Angeles. My career was more stable and making the drive to the San Fernando valley for work wasn't an issue. I was a LA city girl now, and I felt a lot cooler. I was going out in Hollywood and Nyx was coming to visit often for parties or as a stop off point in her many travels. We had a two bedroom with the idea that the second bedroom would be for shooting, but mostly it was a chaotic messy art room that Nyx would live in part time. Her and I's relationship was physically independent from each other, but emotionally we, or at least I, was still deeply enmeshed with her.

It was the same story on repeat. The old me who loved to party and get fucked up and not really care about other people, and the new me I was building that had roots and community. The person who was starting their own company, and in a loving relationship with a man who did not use drugs or alcohol, a person who values health and taking care of their body. I was trying to put the eating disorder days behind me and doing drugs did not help with that.

But man, I sure loved to go out and drink.

I made friends with some people who worked at a major EDM music studio and that became my little crew. They were young people doing cool shit, representing big DJs, photographing events, and even some were big DJs themselves, but the point is, I felt like I was living and breathing creativity. I was the token porn star of the group, and I felt like I fit right in! But after my drunken nights on the town with my new friends I would awake the next day feeling dissatisfied with my relationship with Angel, wishing we could share more of these experiences together.

He said my dissatisfaction was because I was hungover, and honestly that is some wisdom I carry to this day. Yeah, it's true I feel way more emotional after a night of drinking so now I know that's not the best time to discuss big issues. Unfortunately, when I'd bring up how I felt some ongoing distance between us Angel would be quick to remind me I only felt that way after a night out. This angered me and effectively shut down the conversation.

He wasn't wrong, but neither was I. Distance was forming between us, which is ironic since we were now spending more time than ever together. But the deep connection had stopped, the project of creating a production company with me became a duty of business and not something fun we were doing because it gave us joy. And in the background, we were both experiencing major life upheaval.

I had been having near constant problems with my vagina, constant recurrence of bacterial vaginosis, and subsequently having to take antibiotics almost monthly. The doctor just kept prescribing them, and after years of this my gut microbiome was completely fucked up. Constant diarrhea, bloating, craving unhealthy foods yet still turning to them as a form of comfort and because it was easy.

I went to a chiropractor who changed my life. He had been in his profession for over 30 years and used muscle tone testing which revealed that I had a wheat and corn intolerance, as well as aluminum toxicity. I began treatment with supplements he prescribed and stopped eating wheat and corn. I wasn't Celiac, but I'm sure that could have developed if I hadn't gotten my health on track. This forced me to change my entire way of eating and thinking about food.

We found out Angel too had a wheat intolerance but even more scary, had been experiencing priapism which is a boner that won't go down due to drugs like Viagra or the injectables male performers shoot into their dicks, and the only cure is to have a doctor stick a needle in and drain it. His porn career was quickly put into question. Keep taking the boner drugs (as all the guys do) and work, or don't take them, and fail scenes and get fired anyway. He decided to try to continue shooting scenes.

During this time, I also made a terrible mistake, number 3 in my top five if we are counting, by hiring a coke addict to be my site manager and deal with the building and marketing of the site. Everyone I talked to in porn said don't go with mainstream, they will rip you off because you're in porn. Stubbornly, I didn't listen. I was different, I'm not dumb!

Of course, I didn't realize he was on coke and at first, he seemed so legit, overqualified even, but things quickly changed and being young and naive I stayed, and paid him thousands of dollars before realizing he was using it to fund his coke habit. The sunken cost fallacy in full force, I thought if I just held on a little longer, things would work themselves out. I was sure of it. He had been the one to set me up with my website designers and he was going to be the one to run the backend technical aspects of everything, something I know nothing about.

One of the last conversations we had in person was going over marketing materials and as I was listening to him talk to the company we were working with I thought, why are you yelling? Like, I couldn't understand why he was talking so loudly and basically yelling everything he was saying. It was so loud he was hurting my ears, and I was sitting 3 feet from him. It was embarrassing, and confusing, but I didn't know much about coke back then. Sure, I'd done it at parties but never met a true coke addict. And perhaps I was in denial, I needed this to work out, I'd put all my money into it. My pussy couldn't hold on much longer.

Over the course of about 2 years, I put over $25,000 into this project, Hotel LaBeau, the online kinky hotel of your dreams where each door opens another possibility. The website alone cost $7000 and after I fired the corrupt business manager the website went along with it.

The new site developer said he couldn't use the old code and would need to start completely over. $7000 more. Not to mention the time, effort and energy to shoot the scenes, the merchandise I thought was being bought, and whatever amount I had agreed to pay the manager.

Somehow at the end of it all, a dispute over PayPal would be the final straw to break my fucking back. I didn't want it, but they hadn't listened to me and already installed it and were asking me to pay $500 to redo it with the payment processor I wanted. It felt like I was being extorted by my old agency again, having to pay for PayPal after already investing $14000 in a fucking site I had yet to see live was the 6-guy blow bang all over again. If I paid this, what would be the next thing that would hold my site hostage?

My pussy was screaming at me constantly, my friendships felt increasingly hollow, and Nyx and I had a falling out when I told her she couldn't stay at my house anymore because it was getting in the way of my relationship with Angel. And the final blow, that would signify the beginning of the end of my time in the adult industry was what happened with a guy we will call Blake.

I had been working for a company called Kink.com for about 2 years at this point. When I began, I was very excited and wanted to "experience it all."

At kink, before beginning any day there is a protocol that we all have to go through. You sign in, fill out paperwork, and you receive a checklist of your boundaries, wants and desires for the day.

Kink is a BDSM site. If you don't know that acronym, allow me to break it down for you. Bondage and Discipline, Dominance and Submission, and Sadism and Masochism. There are big and subtle differences between all of these categories and every person's interpretation can be slightly different. The goal behind a BDSM scene is to bring the players to a heightened state, by bringing the level of intensity to a place where they feel empowered, not traumatized. Maybe you can't imagine how being tied up and flogged with a whip is empowering. But if you don't know, the best way to learn is to try... with trusted and educated kinksters. The productions at Kink.com were home to some of the topmost educated Doms and Subs in the country and I was lucky enough to get to play with and explore my sexuality with them over the years.

There were dorm rooms at the Armory where performers would stay. It was so magical. Thinking about it gives me such nostalgia for a time that will never come back. I can smell the old building, the brand of cleaner, and the cheap soap and toothpaste provided to all in case we forgot our own. I can feel the softness of black robes each of us were given prior to a scene, becoming a sort of safety blanket between intense acts of BDSM. I can smell the metal on my skin, the sweat, the wood, the rope, the piss and bodily fluids produced from my own body. I can recall the glorious feeling of finishing a super intense scene and going to the showers which were coed, and showering with other performers of all backgrounds, talking about our crazy days, smiling, laughing naked together as we washed off the day. I can feel the bed sheets, feel the marble under my feet, and remember each floor of that gorgeous building. It was so beautiful, and it will never exist in that way again, which makes me sad, but so thankful to have been there during these glory days.

Bruises happened, accidents happened, shitting on people happened. But the environment was always one of openness and non-judgement. Learning about safewords and personal limits and boundaries was paramount, but sometimes these things only happened by realizing that you didn't like a particular something until after it had already happened. An example for me would be that I hate electricity. I discovered this after I was booked consensually for a site called ElectroSluts where the main focus is using electricity. I found out pretty quickly that I did not like it and ended up with a small burn on my vaginal lips after a metal speculum was inserted into my (WET) pussy and a device that had an electric current was used to scare and torture me by shocking the speculum. The burn was minor, healed in a day or two, and an accident I am sure, but it taught me that electricity would always go on my NO list after that. I just don't like the way it feels; I don't like the anxiety it gives me, nothing about it is pleasant to me.

Unfortunately, I did not clarify this knowledge to my agent loudly or quickly enough. What usually happened was at the beginning of the month I would call my agent and normally he just says you're working for Kink these X number of days and then closer to the shoot date I would get an emailed call sheet with the info like the site, your scene partner, flight details, etc. Mark Spiegler at the time was the best agent in the adult biz, no contest. You work hard, you stay very busy, and you don't cause him grief, that's the arrangement.

Upon receiving my call sheet, I had the sinking realization that I was booked again for that site. I knew that he would be upset if I canceled the scene last minute, so I called him said, "Hey, Mark! I hate electricity please don't book me again for that site, I thought I told you before but I'm telling you now." And voila, he never booked me for it again.

But, I still had to do the scene.

I could not have known that after this shoot I would be permanently scarred and afraid of this cruel device called the cattle prod. It's exactly what it sounds like, an electric prod made for cattle. A torture device which makes this high pitch ringing noise when you press the button as it begins to charge. That day I was put through more intense torture than in my whole life. I say torture with all honesty because, I like the thud, I like the dominance and control, I like to suffer beautifully, I do not however, *like* electricity and it took all my training to breathe through moments, I wasn't suffering beautifully, I was just suffering, yet enjoying being able to scream, a lot, I do love to scream. That day I literally screamed until I couldn't scream anymore. But the result was after being cattle-prodded over and over again my brain just said, NO. Never a-fucking-gain do I want to hear that little evil ringing noise or feel that shock, hear that loud snap of electricity as metal prod met soft skin. And I listened to what my body asked for.

I realized later that when the device was even brought out and I heard the noise I would go into a state of panic and shock. That's not normal in BDSM, directors and doms are trained to spot signs of shock and panic and to bring the sub back down to an intense but safe level. Intensity is gradually increased to lessen risk of shock, and for other safety reasons like bruising and mental tolerance. If someone is in shock bad things can happen, they can pass out from accelerated heart rate or breathing, they can have past traumas surface and disassociate, or just generally not have a good time, which is not the goal, not a good thing. I think I can speak for most of the directors at kink and say not one of them wants anyone to go home feeling traumatized or having had a bad day.

Keep in mind, in no way am I some delicate flower that can't take a good beating and use her safe words appropriately. I remember one day being lowered down a little too quickly while in a rope suspension and landing wrong on my knee. RED was yelled out of my mouth before I could even think about it. I am also not going to sit here and say that I haven't been beaten blue at kink and enjoyed every second of it. But, it was CONSENSUAL and done SAFELY. I knew on those days what to expect intensity wise, I had taken appropriate time off of work with Spiegler to allow for healing of bruises, and in one of my most brutal scenes, I actually wrote the script! It was my personal fantasy to explore that I had requested. Kink loves to make fantasies come true and I enjoyed thinking of crazy ideas to ask them to orchestrate. I have so much love for everyone at Kink, and feel they were instrumental in my growth as a person and performer.

I was hired for a site called The Upper Floor. This was one of my favorite sites to work for and often did. They would invite real life kinksters from San Francisco to come to attend this party, sometimes it was a dinner, sometimes a brunch, and they could drink cocktails, eat small bites, and watch a live sex show for their carnal entertainment! They could also "play" with each other. It was real life, live, and completely unique.

And oh my goodness, the decor! The Upper Floor is divine, it's decadent, its luxurious, its bespoke, should I go on? It's a masterpiece living room, dining room, playroom, dream space! And I was a submissive there! I was trained, I was obedient, I had a master and sisters and different Daddies. The feeling of community was real. The people I met at night on the smoking deck during my breaks were some of the most refined and elegant people, true San Franciscans. There was an energy there on The Upper Floor, and it was special.

Before each upper floor party, we were asked if we wanted the public to be able to touch us, or just tested industry people who often attended for fun when they were staying a few days at the Armory for multiple shoots. Even if they weren't hired or paid to participate, they may grope a breast or participate in some way to make the performance more exciting. Or we could choose strictly for the hired talent only to be allowed to touch us. Usually, one man was hired and 2-3 women. I almost always consented to other tested performers being allowed to touch and participate in my live performance, as well as the hired ones of course, but not the audience. Unless it was Public Disgrace, that shit was wild. You'll have to Google it. OK fine, I'll give you the punchline: I was hanging upside down, tied up by my ankles playing bob for dicks as 5 men swung me from dick to dick in a little room called the speakeasy with about 35 audience members watching, fondling, and groping me. Wild.

Blake was there for that scene, as one of the dicks I was bouncing off of, I had worked with him many times at Kink. I had the impression he was like a spoiled prince, who expected people to play along with his games. He had a really immature sense of humor, and at 19 years old I thought he was cool. I'm not talking shit, that will come soon, just read his blogs about "fucking this girl, she's got a cool ass, he ate a burrito" you're getting actually a pretty accurate portrait of the thought processes of Blake. For the most part, I did trust him. I played along with his games, that was the price to pay and I was cool with it, but something changed after a while.

I think I changed. I started porn at 18 and found major success very quickly. I worked constantly, and more so after I signed with Mark Spiegler.

Micro traumas were a daily experience. Hearing jokes that maybe were not that funny, but hey we're in porn, don't be a buzzkill! Recounting stories of other performers and their mishaps, their STDs, their lack of financial savings. Gossip, between the girls, between the agents, the crew, the producers. You could learn a lot if you just listened. And I did. Be sexy but also approachable and cool. Be agreeable but not so agreeable that you let directors get extra for free. Feel free to talk about your wild behavior, your boyfriend problems, your family drama, but don't talk about being burned out or not enjoying sex work. Be the perfect whore, don't make the industry look bad.

After a year and a half of learning the ropes, I had found more strength in myself. I didn't have to play "the game" unless I was getting paid. Some days on porn sets were a test of mind and willpower to maintain the smile and the cheerful attitude, the promise of a big blunt waiting for me at home keeping me going throughout the day. The way I viewed Blake changed, because I didn't *want* to play his game anymore and realized I had a choice. I just put up with him in the moments I needed to, I thought he was annoying but harmless.

Like this joke he would say to me. It started one evening when I was very new at kink still, we ended up down on the bottom level wandering the dark corridors as talent often would. I had never done anal at this point but had experimented with toys. He convinced me to let him slowly put his dick in my ass, so slow. It was amazing in the sense he did it micro inch at a time and honestly, I felt no pain, this is a trick he's used on lots of girls I found out later. But it worked! And before I knew it, he was fucking me in the ass for my first time. It was fine, but I wasn't that into it because I remember being emotionally and physically tired at that point, feeling slightly overwhelmed by this world of sex at every corner. I said to him, "Everyone wants to fuck me." in a resigned and sarcastic tone, his dick still pumping inside me. It is with the same resignation that I say now, I wish I had just kept my overly dramatic mouth shut.

I would continue to hear him say that phrase to me repeatedly throughout my next few years. When he would say it, it made me uncomfortable like it wasn't meant to be nice or empowering. "Everyone wants to fuck you!" he would say, and I would laugh and say yeah, "Everyone wants to fuck me!" Like it was some stupid catchphrase, but it wasn't. It was a reminder of a moment of vulnerability that was used against me and bastardized for his amusement, but no one hearing it would ever suspect that.

Where am I going with all this backstory? Am I avoiding writing about the moment that changed my perspective of Blake, the industry, and myself forever? Am I nervous to go back to that moment and recount my anger, my shock, my sadness? Yes, but I hope this is the last time.

They were hosting a brunch on the Upper Floor, and myself, a male actor I'd worked with a bunch, and I don't even remember which other girls were hired as talent. It's funny the things you remember. The upper floor has a tendency to get a bit crazy. You have real life couples whipping and fucking next to the talent who are fucking, the director leading the show like some circus master, and camera (wo)men at each side of the room trying to capture all the action. This is what I remember vividly about that day. Blake was in attendance as an audience member only. He was drinking alcohol, and I remember the brown colored liquid in his glass, it had ice. I remember I didn't feel safe with Blake anymore, I felt annoyed. I remember that Kink had recently put a new rule in place where if something has been put on your "NO" list that actors can't even bring it out to threaten with. This rule was only a few weeks old. I remember Blake going over and grabbing the cattle prod because gossip had spread that I was absolutely terrified of it, and he thought that would be fun to tease me with. I remember getting really nervous hearing the ringing begin to charge and screaming very loudly, "It's on my NO list!! It's on my NO list!" Knowing that he would be required to put it down, especially because it was a live party with a lot of witnesses, he HAD to comply. I remember him laughing and saying, "OK let's take a look at your No list," which if he wanted to participate, he should have looked at PRIOR to any play. Keep in mind he had been drinking hard liquor at this point and should have not participated in the scene as a professional knowing that that isn't respectful. But we all make exceptions, we value personal autonomy highly. I remember he then proceeded to go down my check list one item at a time. I remember him getting to "face slapping" on my checklist and bringing his hand back and slapping my open mouth extremely hard. I remember feeling a painful cracking sensation from my ear drum to my lower jaw. And then I remember feeling panic as I realized I couldn't close my mouth. I remember the anger I felt as the camera left (don't want to capture anything on camera that could get you sued) and I was surrounded by crew keeping me out of sight of the guests as I cried tears of fear, not enjoyment. I remember Blake never spoke the words, I'm sorry. He said stuff like, "Oh, it's just lock jaw, it's just lock jaw" the people around me repeating the same fucking thing. "Just massage your jaw, it's ok! It's just lock jaw, it's happened to me"

"Fuck all of you!" I wanted to yell at every single one of them and tell them to go fuck themselves and their stupid advice. But I couldn't close my fucking mouth, and I couldn't stop crying. This isn't supposed to happen. You *never* slap someone in the face with their jaw open. If you're going to slap them extra forcefully you *always* cradle the jaw on the other side. KINK BASICS 101! At that time Blake had been in the business for a good 10+ years. He was as experienced then as I am now. He knew better and I never felt he had remorse.

After a while I was finally able to close my mouth, I don't remember how many minutes of massaging and slowly trying to open and close my jaw it took but eventually I could speak. I went into the green room that was for talent only and I told the male actor I was working with, "Keep him away from me. Fucking Blake."

And I dealt with it like anything. I was annoyed but I just shoved it down. Fuck it all. I came home and told Angel what had happened. A few days later he was on a gangbang bang set with Blake as a performer and Blake did the same fucking thing to some lifestyle MILF type (her husband was there watching) and said to the performer while looking at Angel, oh don't worry, just happened to LaBeau last week! Now putting Angel on the spot to participate by omission and agree with him. Which he did.

Barf.

I remember sitting in our bedroom in Koreatown snuggled in bed as he told me this, our mutual understanding of the kind of person he is. Both of us would go on to work for James again after this. Yes, the back bones were weak on us. A big Hollywood movie where I got to make out with Lindsey Lohan? How the fuck could I say no? If this was a bribe, or what's the word, hush money? I was going to take it. I had done scenes with him following the kink scene. During one of them it was so weird because he would barely spank me, like he was overdoing an attempt to tone it down. And in my head, I was like, this scene is lame, you're being lame, why? Then again, I was working with Blake and a second male performer, and the same male actor that had been on The Upper Floor was directing a soft BDSM movie, for couples and the first thing Blake does when the director calls action is walk over, open my eye, and spit in it.

Cut! The director questioned him, dude what are you doing?! This is a soft movie that's more about being beautiful and getting tied up. Everything with him felt like a mind game under the surface. It was exhausting. But people still hired him.

And I couldn't say anything. At that time, he was Golden Boy, he was the star of the Adult world, he was bringing mainstream attention to porn which is something we LOVE. To not work with him would not fly with Spiegler nor really benefit me. 90% of the time scenes with him were fine, but that 10%. I still have issues with my jaw, a constant reminder of how he violated my body.

The "allegations" against him wouldn't come out for a few years, I had no idea I wasn't the only woman he had harmed, though putting the stories together others had told me I should have guessed. He knew who to target, and when. He knew what he could get away with, which towards the end was A LOT. After a good bitching with some girlfriends, and ultimately turning Kink down when they offered medical care, I moved on with my life with a new chip on my shoulder. But my career was at its peak.

Looking back, the mental trauma I was carrying that I had gotten from all the fucked up situations was when I truly felt afraid of the mask. The nice girl mask, the down for anything mask, the pliable and easily manipulated mask, don't want to be rude! I thought we all knew that we were playing a game during scenes, that it's a performance, and he showed me that it was indeed real and there were limits I did not want to ever reach again. I still have jaw issues from this day and part of me wants to go get X-Rays to see what damage was truly done, and I am afraid of what I will find. The proof that I let myself down, I didn't protect myself and ended up with lifelong injuries, for what, or rather, for whom? That's the moment it stopped being fun.

What the fuck did I actually care about in the porn industry? Was any of it real? Anybody actually real? Or were we all just physical avatars of these charters that we only had a part in creating? The fans decide who you are, what our image best represents, and you can play within those boundaries. Don't get tattoos, you'll ruin your girl next door look, keep your hair blonde because that's your brand, and obviously be fit, curvy, or fulfill some kind of niche. Did I really love sex and want to start my own production company because I loved it so much? Part of me did and loved the creativity in producing my own scenes, but the other part saw that I was in a cage and that was one way of escape.

Yet this is the year I appeared in a Movie called *Wasteland*, by Elegant Angel. This was the biggest feature by the biggest company I had ever been in. And I was the co-star with another performer named Lily Carter. And it was an amazing experience to film, the crew, the director, the cast and extras, the locations, you could tell this was their big feature and they were doing it up.

The pressure got to me, a few days before filming I went to a Korean hair salon and completely fucked up the beautiful blonde coloring I'd had done before. All I needed was a touch up but somehow decided to fucking change the whole thing? The process was torture and the whole time I was like, do you literally hate me? And maybe they did because I was a white girl speaking English pulling up to a Korean hair salon. The washing was so forceful, and the bleach was overwhelming and everything just felt off. And I took it, partly because I was just so confused as to what was happening and also holding on to hope I was misjudging the situation. I was not. It looked terrible and my scalp had been beaten up, paying wasn't an issue because it got me the fuck out of there. We had a friend/hair stylist who charged premium Hollywood prices but made house calls and he was able to come over the next night and fix it.

My anxiety was in full swing; I think it's the thing that kept me going every day. Just living in constant stress. My agent being mad at me, the hours of traffic I sat in my car every day, the cost of living in LA and always buying stuff for the next shoot or the next event, I was only breaking even every month and had no clue what savings were or even how to go about getting them. The freedom I got from working independently in the porn industry had cost me the time and ability to develop skills outside of it. That terrified me. I needed to escape, I needed to get out before I couldn't. I needed to live in the real world for a while before I forgot how to. Maybe this is what led to my personal Britney Spears moment.

I had known I was going to shave my head for almost a year, just waiting for a moment when it wouldn't disrupt any shooting. After filming *Wasteland* I was still working consistently but in complete burnout. I could feel my body begging me for a break. When I went home for Christmas of 2012 I let my sister dye my pristine blonde hair a multicolor ocean of blues, teals, and purples. She was so annoyed that I shaved it a few days later. But in my white tiled bathroom in Los Angeles the bright crisp daylight pouring in, every snip felt magical. The bursts of color littering every surface of that white room looked so pretty in contrast.

When it was time to finally take a buzzer and shave it off, I felt so free, so rebellious, so excited to feel that buzz all over my head. And when it was over I absolutely loved it. Shaved head was one of my favorite looks and I think often about doing it again. The only issue being that everyone thinks having a shaved head gives them license to call you Sinead O Conner or Demi Moore or ask if you're sick. It's really weird and I hated the attention, yet I kept my head shaved for over a year.

Wasteland was supposed to be my big break, launching me into performer of the year territory. Instead, I watched my costar and the director fall in love and the movie became somewhat of an homage to her, some of my scenes being cut in the final edit, and now feeling like the supporting actress instead of co-lead. Whatever, we still got nominated for a bunch of awards and I would finally win (tie) for best actress with my co-star at Xbiz. Not AVN. She won at AVN.

This is not to throw shade at her or the director, it's to express my profound disappointment. I could see what was happening and all I could do was accept it, even be happy for them. Who am I to stand in the way of true love? She would leave the industry after this movie never to be seen again. And honestly, she told me she was going to do that and I'm happy for her. The point is, even the moment that was supposed to be my big time to shine just felt like another instance of feeling hopeful and then disillusioned. The movie would win best movie of the year, best director, best cinematography, but none of those awards belonged to me. I was proud of what we made, and I showed up enthusiastic and supportive of my cast and crew.

But inside I was fucking done.

It was time for me to take care of myself. When I told Angel I was thinking about moving back to Washington, temporarily, he was neutral, understanding, and didn't put up any kind of protest or fight. Before I completely made up my mind I told Spiegler I wanted to do this dance program at The International Dance School of Hollywood but couldn't cover the complete upfront cost and he loaned me the portion I couldn't cover. I thought that was so generous of him, and maybe he could see I was burning out, maybe he hoped this would get me back on track. 5 days a week for 5 hours a day we were dancing. Ballet, jazz, modern, choreography, hip hop, and stretching. I was in heaven!

Taking the metro to Hollywood Blvd and Sunset every day and making friends with the other students in the program, I felt like a normal girl! All I had to think about was dance and how I could move my body in new and challenging ways. It was so healing to reconnect with my body in that way. Something about being in balance, having to do all the exercises on both sides, I remember one night accidentally rolling my joint the opposite way I normally do. I think my brain was enjoying doing things on both sides and wanted balance.

And still, I had to work, I did a few scenes a month to stay afloat and managed to get my certificate when the 3-month program was over, even though I freestyled my choreography routine. I made some friends in the program, but only stayed in touch with one of them. The point of taking this intensive wasn't to become a famous dancer or even a professional dancer. Though I had wanted to create a feature dancing show and have always loved dancing, this was a way for me to hone my skills but more importantly reconnect with my body, joyously, with love.

But 3 months of dancing couldn't undo the 3 years of constant stress I'd put myself through and eventually the load was too much. I inevitably still broke. I couldn't do it anymore. And I quit. I literally said fuck it all. I was out of money and out of the energy it would require making more, as well as trust that it would even work out. I just wanted to go home to my mommy and lick my wounds and sleep for 10 years. In my mind I was a failure. I hadn't won anything, my production company was a bust, I was broke, my friendships had mostly disappeared, and I was tired of playing Lily. I wanted to be Lacy again. So, at age 23 and only 4 years into my porn career, I took my first retirement.

But the monster I'd created would continue to haunt me. There was no getting rid of Lily.

Cosplaying Normal

When I told my mom I wanted to come home she was all too happy to help. The different reactions to my family finding out about my career were all performatively nice, but hollow. One aunt named her dog Lily and at a family function told me the dog's full name was Lily… Lily *LaBeau*, said with a tone of sickly-sweet condescension. At that point no one had explicitly said anything about my career but after a few years I realized they had all found out.

Or at least I thought everyone knew.

My dad found out in probably the worst way possible. At his local bar that he would frequent weekly, one of the young guys came with a Hustler magazine which I was in and showed my dad in front of all his buddies. Look, Harold! Your daughter is in Hustler!

Looking back, I wish I had told him myself, but his reaction was what I thought it would be. Screaming, wishing me dead.

Spiegler has a joke, tell your parents you're wanted for murder, then tell them no actually I'm just doing porn. The disassociation was real as I listened to my dad scream at me and tear into every fiber of my soul, "I wish you had murdered someone! Anything but this! Anything!"

I thought, "Well, I guess Spiegler's little trick wouldn't have worked."

When I had started dipping my toes in the modeling world at 15 my aunts didn't want to help with the costs to attend a John Robert Powers modeling weekend, saying that modeling would lead me to porn. My mom couldn't afford the classes on her own, so I needed their help to attend. I believe in the end they did eventually give us the money we were short.

My dad was super excited about me modeling and was proud of my beauty. And so, I think when he found out that I had indeed gone into porn it was embarrassing and felt like a big fat I told you so by all the family to him. Still the favorite scapegoat, they could now have another reason for reproach.

The underlying message: if you had been a better father this wouldn't have happened.

When I came home for a visit after they found out, no one asked me questions, or cared to go too far into details, but they all said the same thing which was funny to me at the time. "If ever you need somewhere to stay, you're welcome at mine." It didn't feel loving, it felt like, when you finally break down and have nothing left you can give us the validation of saving you, but only temporarily because we all have lives outside of you.

There would be a few times where I actually did need help, and they were not there, sometimes not even responding to my texts, even to say no, sorry we cannot help. Just, nothing, no response at all. The loudest messages in my family are always the ones spoken behind your back.

Maybe that's why I fall for the flatterers, the ones with the right things to say in the moment but no follow through or action accompanied with it. I've waited years for change, believing what someone said to me and disregarding the actions they continuously showed. That's love, isn't it?

Or is love rescuing like my mom would teach me? Instead of believing in me and allowing me to work things out on my own it wasn't more than a few months between me saying I wanted to leave LA and her arriving with the then boyfriend of my sister in a U-Haul to drive me back up to Washington.

Angel never protested, even helped me get my things together. I was still somehow believing that it would only be temporary. That I was just going home to get back on track, I would return to LA soon. I told Angel this wasn't a breakup, simply a break. And I actually believed it.

Porn gave me structure, Spiegler gave me professionalism, being on set and going to the events gave me community, Angel gave me love and comfort, and within 2 days of driving I said goodbye to all of it and moved into the tiny spare bedroom of my mom's little house in Everett, Washington.

My sister had her first baby in 2009, the same year I had started porn. I had taken a few months off when she had her first baby to help her when she had to return to work. I never thought I wanted kids, but that little dude changed everything. He was so moody, and would cry endlessly, and peed on me, and I loved him more than anything I've ever loved in my life.

By the time I moved back to Washington, Orla was now onto her 2nd baby, a precious little redhead who absolutely loved me, her auntie. I can't explain why we had such an instant bond, but whenever she and I were together she was either in my arms or on my lap. My sister's son had let me hold him and trusted me enough to sleep in my arms, but I could never replace his mom. Our bond was nothing like the little girl that came after.

Kids don't care if you're a whore, they care how you treat them. In essence they're easy. Give them food, love, cuddles, entertainment and they will give you the purest love you've ever had. They test your patience, and I can look back at my younger self and regret the times I lost my temper or didn't have the patience to be an adult when that's what was needed of me. In a way we were all growing up together. I hope to be blessed with children of my own someday and I am so thankful for the gift of these beautiful souls that I get to witness grow up.

The plan was to move back in with my mom and rely on camming and freelance modeling to provide an income. Except, I forgot I hated camming, I was terrible at managing my own schedule, and my mom was more than happy to host me for free, so I didn't need to struggle. At the time I was more than happy to let her.

I've always loved my independence, and the relationship between my mom and I had varied from totally enmeshed and codependent, to me being completely independent and not seeing her at all during those first few years in the industry. I carried guilt for that and there was a part of me that felt like the prodigal daughter coming home.

Everyone seemed so happy I was back in Washington, and I had to show them that I was still me! I was still normal! Sure, I'd fucked like hundreds of men and women and done crazier shit than they could ever fathom, traveled all over the world and had my heart broken into pieces a few times, but I'm still just a silly little goof still. My self-esteem was so low, but I couldn't take a moment to think about it and definitely couldn't let anyone else know that!

Porn failure or not, my thirst for adventure and a good time had not died, if anything, now 22, it increased dramatically. Going out to our favorite gay bar in Everett, making the drive to Seattle for nights out in the city. Hangovers were a regular part of my weekends, and my sister would invite me over to cuddle with her kids when I was feeling like dog shit. There's nothing better for a hangover than baby cuddles she'd tell me.

She was right. There's really nothing better in this world than baby cuddles.

The first few months I continued talking to Angel. We were just separated, not finished, I said, lying to him and myself. I made a trip to LA, head shaved, needing money. My "retirement" had not lasted long. Porn was what I knew, and Spiegler was ok with me coming for a few weeks/months at a time, he even allowed me to sleep at his house, for a fee, and would book me work.

On my first trip back to LA, I remember Angel came over to Spiegler's house where I was staying and we talked casually about life, avoiding anything too deep or uncomfortable. Inside my feelings for him were gone. He felt like a stranger to me, and as he was saying goodbye, he went to give me a kiss and instinctively I turned my head away. I couldn't kiss him, but I couldn't be a fucking adult and say straight out to his sad looking face that we were over, and he couldn't say the words out loud to confirm what he must have known to be true.

I thought we both understood at that moment.

The trip passed like any other and soon I was back in Washington for the holidays. Spending them with my dad's family and with my mom and sister. They were good times overall, but I was still fragile mentally and suffering with my ongoing eating disorder as well as food allergies so my moods could fluctuate. The guilt I felt for the times I lost my cool, the embarrassment of how easily my close family triggered me, I was so ashamed of myself.

A friend of mine from my partying days with The Internationals at ASU in Arizona reached out to me and as luck would have it, we were living only 10 minutes from each other! He and his brother had been living with their parents, and they were a 420 friendly household. He also knew about my work and was unfazed. It was nice to be around someone who had known me before the industry.

I'd spend so much time at their house, my friend and his brother were two wild boys. They loved to do crazy shit, party, and make music. Even if I wasn't into rap, I was into creating and we would have so much fun hanging out in their basement while they would record music in their little DIY sound booth they had built.

I was also still writing music but hadn't found the confidence in my own voice yet to really do anything serious with it. We made music videos and my friend's brother and I would flirt casually but nothing happened at first because he was in the process of ending his previous (now long distance) relationship.

But end they did, and eventually Max and I would have sex in the basement of his parents' house when no one was home, and it was amazing, he was so sensitive and sweet and really knew how fuck. We made a video for this site called Make Love Not Porn which Angel and I had also uploaded to.

I wasn't trying to do anything cruel, I was confident at this point Angel and I were over and it was time to move on. In his novel, Angel said that it wasn't until he saw our video that he realized our relationship was truly done. I had not wanted to hurt Angel. I should have been explicit, yet he had not been either. The reason Angel and I "never fought" was because we were both deeply conflict avoidant. And I think that's why the spark died. We never practiced healthy conflict, preferring to live in a little bubble and close our eyes and ears from anything that threatened it, not realizing this was our doom.

Max was the opposite. He had what I'd describe as a major anxiety disorder, having gone through serious traumatic events that began in his childhood. He would have anxiety attacks and explained to me that once he'd gone to the hospital with a seizure from so much anxiety. I have big feelings too, I understand!

I thought that I was the perfect person for him. He reminded me of my dad, and I thought I could be the safe loving space that would allow him to feel safe and to heal. Instead, I became more and more anxious. If I didn't respond to a gift the way he wanted or a grand gesture he surprised me with he would get upset with me and we'd talk about it for hours while waiting for his heightened nervous system to calm down. There was no room for me to have big feelings, I needed to stay loving and calm even if inside I was shrinking. I learned to keep things clean as he couldn't stand a mess and was always trying not to set off his anxiety.

It was so hard when we fought because I'd start to defend myself and he would say he was getting so upset he felt a seizure coming so I was forced to shut up or be the fucking monster that sent her boyfriend to the hospital. Our relationship was codependent, and it was toxic but at least it kept my mind off of my own perceived failures.

Max was also really cool about my work in the beginning. He didn't care if I shot scenes and our agreement was that whatever happens on set was fine, but I wouldn't engage with performers off set. This was basically the same agreement I'd had with Angel, and it felt fair. For a while it worked. But the fights and anxiety continued regardless. We became the on again off again couple and I can't count how many times we broke up and got back together.

During one of our breaks, Nyx had invited me out to Amsterdam to stay in her new place. She was in the process of immigrating over there and was totally in love with the lifestyle. I wasn't unfamiliar with Europe at this point, but Amsterdam was somewhere I'd never been. She made it sound idyllic and dreamy.

Absolutely broke and exhausted from life in Washington, it was time for Nyx to host me, and we were excited to be reunited again. Amsterdam in the summer is a magical place to be. As soon as I got there one of her friends presented me a basic but usable bike he'd bought off a crackhead. I guess this is a common thing in AMS. There's more bikes than people and when crackheads get desperate, they either steal or sell their own bike for a cheap price.

Didn't seem ethical but who was I to judge a different culture? The day I arrived we went to Albert Heinz and I bought a bottle of rosé and a beet salad and we sat on the edge of one of the canals and enjoyed my happy arrival. They took me to a place called Hill Street Blues, one of the oldest and most famous weed coffee shops in the city. I discovered my love of fresh peppermint tea with honey, and we sat with 5 or 6 of Nyx's new friends smoking splifs.

I was a pothead but usually when you smoke in a circle you're passing 1 joint around. Each friend had rolled their own joint and there were 3-4 being passed around the table. As soon as I passed one, another was placed in my hands. This was my dream come true! The sun was shining, everyone was laughing, you could even hear the birds chirping through the big open windows that looked out onto the canal waters just beyond the graffiti covered walls.

But then, suddenly my ears started ringing. I'd passed out before and could feel the tunnel vision beginning. "I'm gonna pass out I managed to mumble to the table" "drink Coca Cola!! Your blood sugar is low, you need to drink sugar!" I tried to take a sip of the fizzy brown drink that had been placed in front of me but was too weak to move and then everything went black.

Suddenly I was on my hands and knees on the hardwood floor projectile vomiting beets and rosé all over the fucking place. It was actually kind of pretty because it was a lovely shade of maroon, but upon realizing what had just happened I was mortified. The girls quickly ushered me into the bathroom and one of Nyx's friends, Tom, was kind enough to clean my vomit off the floor. A little later everyone would tell me their stories about when they got way too high their first time. Amsterdam is not for children, and this was my warning from the universe: *pace yourself.*

Those three months did not pass without difficulty. Nyx and I's relationship wasn't what it used to be and there was still a lot of emotional enmeshments. She was very independent and was getting frustrated with me being in her space so often. It was also not very easy for me to make money and so I couldn't go out and spend frivolously on whatever I wanted.

A friend of hers had offered to introduce me to one of their regulars, a client her friend would see in person. I hadn't done much escorting at that point, but I was ok with what was offered. Though she didn't specify how much he'd pay I knew what she said he had given her and was fine with it. However, when the job was over and I unraveled the notes, he'd place in my had right before leaving, my heart sank.

$200?

But it was supposed to be triple that?

I was so disappointed, and angry and told the friend that this was fucked up and to confront him. But no sympathy was directed my way, it was more important to keep him as a client then to stand up for me and get more money. After that, I ended up staying with Tom. He'd been flirting with me the whole time, but I really wasn't sexually attracted to him.

He was a porn super fan and adored whores and marijuana.

I could tell he was a nice guy, or at least wanted to be, but I was another whore to be pursued and then conquered. So, I dodged his explicit requests when they would arise. And enjoyed the moments of friendship in between.

He was happy to host me, smoke me out, and allow me to cook and clean for him. It was a nice arrangement, and we had fun going out together. One night he asked me if I wanted to try speed, and I was like, why not? He placed a pharmaceutical looking pill in my hands, and I thought maybe he's calling it speed but it's like Adderall or something. Whatever I took, it made me feel energized, wild, a bit animalistic and when we came home, my defenses were down, and my crazy girl was in full power. I finally caved and gave Tom a BJ.

I wasn't interested in anything sexual, but the stars aligned, and he got one of my famous thank you blow jobs. When I'm fucked up and dudes are really nice to me, I sometimes suck their dick to say thank you.

Things were turning up because I had been offered to be flown out to Cancun, Mexico to attend this rich white dude's week-long sex party as an escort. There was a base rate of $10,000 for the trip and extra money for each additional sex act performed with the guys. I'd never done anything like that, and it did make me nervous, but the money was too good to pass up.

Being a professional whore, I made sure I got tested before this because to me it was like another porn scene. Wanted to make sure I was good to go and as luck would have it AMS had a free STD testing for sex workers. It was so easy and streamlined and made me realize how expensive and difficult they make STD testing for people in the United States.

I hopped on a plane and found myself in Cancun and me and 3 other girls were driven to the villa where everyone would be staying, we got in late at night and mostly everyone went to bed. Before I could even unpack my bag, I received my test results back from my STD test. Gonorrhea of the throat only.

Tom!!!!

You god damn mother fucker!!!!!

Fuck!!!

I couldn't sleep after that and sat outside listening to the waves until the sun came up and the organizer of this event would be awake to talk to. It was beautiful that morning, thank God because the knot in my stomach was not. Not only did I lose out on $10,000 and a week in Cancun, I also had to go back to AMS and to Nyx again with no fucking money.

The organizer was kind when I told him what I'd found out and to say thank you for not just keeping quiet and spreading gonorrhea to 30 people and their unsuspecting wives, he gave me 2k and sent me on the next available flight back to AMS. Word spread and the looks from the girls varied from apathy to disgust as I made my walk of shame out of the villa.

That 2k was enough to pay back Nyx for any money she'd given and contribute to the household and food. But it went fast and pretty soon I was needing more. I'd worked in Budapest before and thought it wouldn't be an issue to go again so I contacted the old agent I had out there, and she booked me a little over a week's worth of work.

One of my first scheduled BG scenes was for a big-name male porn star at his compound. It was like a 10-year-old was given a million dollars and told to create his dream home. Every kind of motorized toy you could imagine all housed in a giant warehouse with other expensive and large toys. The girl I was working with didn't speak much English, so we didn't talk before the scene. But the male actor did and seemed to be good friends with the director.

Before we started, the actor made some off hand joke referencing cocaine and while I was annoyed at the idea of him doing drugs before a scene, I didn't have the power in this situation to say anything. Plus, I wasn't 100% positive that he was using it that day on set, it was just a joke, right?. I really needed this money.

However, 5 minutes into the scene I felt I had my answer. The way he was fucking and how rough he was being with me, bending me too far backwards, holding me in difficult positions and fucking like an animal on meth, in my head I was trying to just get through it.

At some point the male actor bent over and asked me to lick his asshole, something I was fine with but as I put my face down between his cheeks, I saw a cauliflower winking back at me. I immediately stopped, my heart pounding and sick to my stomach. What is that? I asked both the actor and Rocco. It looks like fucking warts on his ass hole.

The director, who was filming, stopped the camera and asked the actor to bend over. Aww man you gotta get that shit burned off, he said to my costar. All while this fucking girl is sitting there with no idea what was going on. She probably didn't even want to be there in the first place. She was an Eastern European girl and a lot of them do porn out of survival making in a few days what would take their entire family months to make. Sometimes they've been pimped out, had their passports taken away, and literally sex trafficked. Europe has a far bigger problem with illegal sex trafficking in their porn industry than the US and it's actually super fucked up how little they give a shit for Eastern Europeans. There is a lot of discrimination.

I'm not sure why or how this girl ended up here, but I don't think she was trying to be the next Jenna Jameson, she just wanted to get through the day, get paid and go home. The director asked me if I would continue the scene and since we were halfway through, exposure had already happened, and no one would get paid if I said no, we finished the scene. Afterwards, the director thanked me for being so professional and gave me 600Euros cash.

I was told that a driver would pick both me and the other girl up from the set and bring me back to the apartment I was staying in. I was wearing a skintight tank dress that barely covered my ass with no underwear to let my pussy breath after that very intense and rough shoot, but as the driver stopped in the middle of the city and told me to get out, I was both confused and horrified.

I thought you were taking me all the way to my apartment?

No English. Get out. And then he handed me my shoot bag and drove away.

What a humiliation ritual. Trying to keep my dress from riding up while walking through the city trying to figure out the nearest public transport, calling my agent to complain and ask what to do. She sent her driver to come get me. I remember the pain I felt in my entire body when I got back to the apartment. Like I'd been hit by a truck. I've done hundreds of rough scenes, but this guy had no restraint, and I still had poor boundaries, my mentality was always, just get through it.

It was hard to move, to stand, to even lay down and sleep. The girl I was staying with, Gina Gerson, was kind and offered me some no-nonsense friendship for the evening. She encouraged me not to cancel the rest of my trip, but I'd already decided. I had to do my scene the next day, even though I felt so dirty and sore. I wasn't sure if they were even warts, maybe they were hemorrhoids? It all happened so fast and obviously there was no ass licking after that… but the damage was done, and my anxiety was in full force.

But my agent had paid up front for my travel, and I had to at least make enough to pay her back. So I worked the next day, settled my dues with her and canceled the rest of my trip and returned to Amsterdam once again, feeling so broken and embarrassed.

Why couldn't I just get through it? Why couldn't I just finish and come back successful? Why was I such a fuck up? Nyx seemed annoyed with my lack of ability to make any money, and we had a few heated conversations about it. She was also struggling with money but had a few gigs to keep her going, and I think the pressure of me being there felt like an added burden to her.

She would eventually write me a letter listing all the reasons she didn't want to be my friend anymore. They seemed so ridiculous to me, like the fact I fall asleep easily and I don't like to party until sunrise and basically that I'm not as fun as I used to be. The list was long and had transgressions she had been holding onto for years. Everything she didn't like about me covered the entirety of our friendship. It wasn't meant to lead to a conversation; it was meant as a goodbye. And she was right. We were becoming two very different people, or maybe I just wasn't trying to be a carbon copy of her anymore, so she was ok discarding me.

Slowly I was finding my own life and way of living, and it turns out I'm nothing really like her. When I met her at 16, I thought she was the fucking coolest and wanted to be just like her. She is the reason I got into the porn industry. I wanted to impress her, be cool like her, show what a bad girl I could be. I started shooting in porn and then she followed. Without her I would have never even thought about this path. Do I feel resentment for that?

At some points in my life, yes.

And I take responsibility that ultimately it was me who agreed to go to Miami. It was me who moved to LA. It was me who decided to do this work and it was me who decided to do it as best as I possibly could. She was the catalyst, but I took full control of the reins and didn't look back.

It was also me who decided to fall in love with it; the good and the bad that came along with it were closely intertwined.

Porn is my career, my expertise, my life's work. So what's the point of regret now? This is my path in this lifetime, and Nyx was there for the beginning of the journey. She gave me confidence to be weird, she showed me how to be a bitch, we had moments where we cried together holding the other tightly in our arms, sisters. I loved her deeply, and she was exactly who I needed during those early years. For that, I can't help but be thankful.

At the end of our friendship, around the time I was 23, I only wanted to be myself. I just hadn't quite figured out who I was yet.

I returned home to Washington after 3 months in Amsterdam.

Back in Washington, back in my normal life, back with Max and our rollercoaster relationship, I somehow got approved for a little basement apartment smack dab in the middle of mine and Max's parents' house and then approved by a furniture company for a couple grand worth furniture and a TV. We moved in together and did our best to play happy couple.

But the fights when they happened, which was every week or two, were getting more and more intense. After some of them I was so dysregulated, I'd begun self-harming again. Hitting my arms, my thighs, punching the concrete backed walls until my knuckles bled. I was a lot better at hiding it though because I was not constantly performing in scenes for porn. Bruises, cuts, and scrapes were easily camouflaged with clothing or make up. It was my shameful secret.

It was a shitty apartment and when fall and winter came so did the mildew smell. Everything in the house took on the smell of mold. Not a fun, bodega-slightly-mildewy-cleaning smell, but this is going to make you sick mold smell. If I close my eyes, I can still smell it, on every piece of clothing, the couch, our bags, skin, hair, everything. Max tried his best, but his anxiety was a fucking monster that would attack without warning. House is clean but the dishes aren't done when he came home? He was screaming at me. I began walking on eggshells and then getting to the point I couldn't take it anymore. The screaming fights became two sided and I screamed back. And it felt good.

Fuck you, dad!

I mean, Max!!

I'm not a little girl anymore and I can be just as much of a psychopath as you if you back me into a corner. He was never ever physically violent, but God I hope I never hear myself scream at someone like that ever again. His brother had moved into the second bedroom and there was a morning where they both were yelling at me. Why? I can't remember! Why do toxic couples fight? I was so sick of it I opened the door in the bedroom shirtless, baring my breasts and soul and screamed back at both of them at the top of my lungs. I was 3 again, veins popping out of my forehead, body shaking and my naked breasts flailing wildly with every exaggerated movement.

I'd been inspired from an article I'd read of some tribal women who did this to remind men that they were women. They looked shocked and it seemed to get my point across. You're two men yelling at one woman blocking the only exit out of the fucking bedroom.

My neighbor had knocked on the door when they had left to make sure everything was ok. The same neighbor we all suspected of beating his wife and keeping her high on drugs and alcohol throughout her pregnancy, with children who themselves look disheveled and dirty. He gave me a cigarette and wished me luck.

I thought to myself, I need to get out of this hell hole. But it would take me time. Max and I had a really good way of working together and he filled the role too well. He would shoot my content for me and even perform with me sometimes and was a pretty good performer. If only each day didn't end in a fight.

We were both sane enough to admit to ourselves and each other that this dynamic was not sustainable. I know in Max's heart he's a decent human, but his anxiety issues and lack of healing from traumas in his past was like living with two separate people. And being around him, I was reverting more and more back into a childlike state that I thought I'd outgrown. He was retraumatizing me, and I was becoming scared of myself.

I'd left his house and was staying in an Airbnb in the city and everything just hit me. The fighting, the pain, the loneliness, the ostracization; I took the edge side of my cell phone and used it to hit my forearm as hard as I could over and over. I needed the external pain to be more than the internal but inside I was in so much fucking pain.

The bruises I left after that were gruesome even to me. I'd hit some vein or something and my entire forearm was black and blue and green and yellow, and I was worried I'd fractured the bone in my right hand from hitting my forearm so hard. That's why I switched to the phone.

Talk about shame.

It wasn't just Max I was angry at, it was myself. It was the 10 fucking green juices I had to throw away because I'd had the great idea to start a juicing business and bought all the equipment for it and decided to try out recipes while staying in temporary home. I had bought too much produce, and I had an excess of juices that no human could consume in a 48-hour period. Am I literally fucking stupid?

I was mad at Nyx and all my friendships that had disappeared when I left LA, I was mad at my fucking mom and sister and our codependent never ending issues, I was mad at my family and the cheerful holograms they projected that disappeared the moment I reached my hand out to touch them, I was mad at my failed loved life, but most of all, I was so mad at myself. I fucking hated myself.

Patreon,

Failure.

Camming,

Failure.

Health,

Failure.

Why couldn't I get my life together!? Why did I have to make everyone's life harder including my own? Why was I such a fuck up? I felt like an idiot and honestly, I wanted to give up. But we (my body, heart, and soul) were past suicide ideation. I may self-harm but I was determined to keep going. The self-harming wasn't to die, it was so I could keep living, it separated me just enough from my own dark thoughts, the adrenaline temporarily pushing out the sadness, the shame giving me something to focus on, to hide, so I didn't have to think about more painful things.

But I could see after this last attack on myself that I may do something one day out of this anger towards myself that could leave permanent damage. If I didn't get help, this path I was going down would not end well for me.

After that night, I reached out to a therapist and committed to a 9-month therapeutic coaching program with a beautiful and spiritual woman. She would encourage me to get my GED since I'd never graduated high school, she would help me connect back with my own spirituality and connection to God, and after those 9 months I was starting to feel like a whole new person.

I'd had this gnawing feeling in my chest for a while that I couldn't shake. It was like a physical calling to me, pulling me with a rope of curiosity and joy. I would spend hours on Google searching for different programs thinking of schemes that would allow me to satisfy this need, this hunger.

Panama.

I was 24 now and not living under the confines of Spiegler and the industry, and realized that I had the ability to do whatever I fucking want. And I wanted to learn more about permaculture. I've had a dream my whole life of having my own farm and retreat center and I thought learning about permaculture would be a great first step towards that dream. I would sit at night and research different farms and volunteer programs and the joy I felt was like a million butterflies flying around and through my body. I could barely sit in my seat while looking at the photos of jungles and tropical beaches. I was so excited.

During this time, Max and I had been able to be friends, despite everything, and he'd help me with shooting my content and sometimes I'd let him use my car. We both understood too well that as a couple we were toxic but as friends we collaborated nicely.

When I found the permaculture program I thought would be perfect for me, I put a little Amazon wish list together and some friends and extended family purchased me basics like, new hiking shoes and work pants since I'd be doing farming in the jungle while I was there. They all rallied around me, and I felt successful again! Finally, something they could be proud of!

This was something they could brag to people about, you know, talk about at the dinner table. If you take off my makeup and put me in street clothes I look like the sweetest of the sweet normal girls. I took my cosplay very seriously and was sure this would be the next major focus of my life.

On the day I was scheduled to leave from Seattle to Panama City, I was definitely nervous. It was one thing to go to Panama at 14 with my mom and family and people who spoke Spanish, it was another to go by myself. I arrived in Panama City, and my host had arranged a taxi for me for the 3-hour drive east to the farm. It was pouring buckets when I got there, and I'd never driven in so much rain before. I couldn't see 3 feet ahead of us, but the driver was not concerned, and drove normally like he was a seasoned pro.

When I arrived at the farm it wasn't quite what the website had described. The days of multiple volunteers and big community farm projects were over, I was there as a social media and photographer as well as farm helper. We were building a permaculture park in a very poor city.

My host was kind, but he was old, physically and mentally and would say racist and sexist things without hesitation, like many of the older generation do. He had no idea about my past, and I had no fucking reason to tell him. I was there to learn about permaculture, and film the updates for the park project, not to spread the gospel of porn.

He thought I was a model and that's all he needed to hear. It fits, I'm pretty, and he treated me kindly. I stayed for 2 weeks on the farm on my first trip, and on my final night I stayed in Panama City. I made friends with some peace corps people at the hostel who had just returned from their own life changing jungle experiences and found myself with a big crush on one of them, and we all went out and did karaoke.

It was my first time doing karaoke and I sang Rick Astley because Rick rolling was a thing, and I wanted to Rick Roll the world. I had been carrying a tiny gel tab of acid in my purse for months and asked the group if they wanted me to put it in the bottle of liquor we were all sharing. They enthusiastically said yes. The effects were light but we all felt the euphoria and sparkles of the neon lights.

Finally, the guy I liked made a move on me but our make out session was cut off when the guard in the alley told us to knock it off. We finished the night and as I lay on the couch in the hostel, not wanting to be too comfortable so I didn't sleep through my alarm. I was trying to get a few hours of sleep before my 5am taxi, and he decided that was when he would try to continue the session from earlier.

And he was really annoying about it; I was like dude, I gotta sleep before my flight. I was exhausted. But he kept asking, nicely but persistently and I was like, no. I'm fucking tired. But I'll be back in Panama in a few months and so will you. But the conversation dried up quickly upon my return home, and it became clear he was just looking for a hook up that night.

I was really disappointed but had become used to this sort of behavior from men now and accepted it. The friend group he was a part of was welcoming to me and so I decided I'd rather have a group of friends then be mad at some dude for being overly horny.

I would return for another 2 weeks a few months after that and on my second trip I'd meet another farm worker that was a part of the project, a young man who was also interested in learning permaculture and it was nice to have a friend close to my age. It was so nice to be working, digging, planting. You always have something interesting to talk about with people who love nature.

The jungles were just as beautiful and otherworldly as I had remembered and I would walk around the farm eating fruit off the trees and talking in the scenery. The 90-degree days and the constant humidity was perfect for me, as someone with dry skin and naturally curly hair I feel like I'm made for tropical climates. I never feel alone when I'm surrounded with that much natural beauty, and to me, Panama is one of the most beautiful places in the world.

I also decided at the end of my stay on that second trip that I was going to live full time in Panama and had toured an apartment in the city and been accepted to rent. I was so excited that night and was running around with the other farm worker and was about to leap across the intersection when I heard my friend call my name from behind. Lacy!! I stopped to look back at him and when I turned forward a second later a bus was barreling straight through where my body should have been.

We looked at each other laughing due to shock. Did I almost just die?

He said to me, wanna hear something trippy? In a parallel dimension you just did.

Near death experience aside, I loved being in Panama. It was dangerous, wild yet there were a lot of anti-white-American vibes cast my way, but I was optimistically happy. The islands and beaches, the waterfront, my developing Spanish language skills, the nature! I was finding my rhythm and where the younger people hang thanks to my new peace corps friends and couldn't wait to get back and move into my new apartment in the city.

The boys didn't know what to do with me out there. They fell in love fast, and I hated to break their hearts. I wished we could just be friends, but those days were long gone. Most men I met, whatever age, had no desire to be my friend. They wanted to fuck me, or marry me and if I didn't reciprocate that desire, they found no reason to stay in my life. And that's ok, because I value the moments knowing that they all eventually end. Skinny dipping in the Panama Pacific, a wild night of making out and cuddling together, yet I didn't want to have sex, and that confused them so much.

Maybe I shouldn't have done anything with them, been a chaste prude and had better boundaries. I didn't. I had so much fun experimenting with this feminine energy. I liked flirting, I liked being liked, I liked the connection while it lasted.

One night, a new friend of mine and I were doing coke during a party and every time we went in the backroom together to take bumps, he would beg me to fuck him or suck his dick. I didn't want to, not even a pity BJ, but ending up wrapping his belt around his neck and making him go on all fours like a dog. He loved it.

Eventually I stroked his dick, he looked so cute and pathetic staring up at me, big puppy eyes. It was more fun to tease him, to see the desperation and excitement in his eyes, to spit on his cock but never let him feel my lips wrapped around it. I loved it.

The next morning, I received a call from Spiegler. A company in the UK was having horrible luck with people cancelling or getting stopped at the border and they wanted to know if I could fly out and shoot in London.

Hell fucking yes, I could! I love calls like that.

So, the next day I flew straight from Panama City, Panama, to London for the first time in my life. I'd always wanted to visit there, and it was so exciting to be going for work. It also happened to be a good friend of mine's 40th birthday and the schedule was timed perfectly so that I could attend.

The scene was with Adriana Chechik who I had always wanted to work with. She was the embodiment of a porn star and so beautiful and kind. The shoot days were cold and long but the movie was made with such attention to detail. I played the part of Phasma, and my outfit was a replica storm trooper suit, painted to match my character.

Did I feel sexy in it? Not at all. Did I know that all the Star Wars fans would absolutely die of happiness when they watched the movie?! Yes! The attitudes on set were positive, and we all had a nice time hanging out together at our hotel before and after our long shoot days. I love traveling with other performers, it's so easy to get along as most are very friendly and since we all get it we can talk shop, reminisce about the past, and talk about our lives without judgement.

The trip passed quickly and soon I was leaving with a bit more money and freshly made memories from a country that was as beautiful as I had always dreamed it would be.

I flew back to Washington to spend the holidays with my family and at the end of December packed my life into 2 large suitcases and made the move to Panama. I was enrolled in a Spanish language school, and I had a nice little group of people to hang out with and many adventures ahead of me. I was still working for the farmer and on the project, but I was also just enjoying my grandmother's country. She was still alive at this time, and my goal was to find someone familiar with the country and brave enough to travel into the Darien jungle to accompany me to visit Maria.

I had contact with 1 family member, my grandmother's nephew but he was busy with his own life and family matters. My requests never seemed that important to him and I didn't want to push. So, I spent my days traveling with friends to different beaches and even had friends come to stay with me for a few weeks. Panama is magical, it's wild, it's in constant construction, the skyscrapers giving the appearance of a grand metropolis but on the streets, you could still feel the economic and cultural differences from other developed countries I'd been to.

This was the first time I'd see a real-life slum. It was incomprehensible and horrifying and completely accepted by the people outside of it. There was money in Panama, but it was for a very select few. Most people were middle class or poor, or extremely poor. I saw it all.

There was an understanding that it was important to keep myself safe when I was there. I was not that naive, but I was young, and so curious and excited to soak up all the sights, smells, tastes, and midnight salsa dancing sessions while drinking Abuelo Rum and laughing with my friends.

Time passed and we finished the permaculture park and I was simply learning to live my new life there, but my assimilation didn't feel quick enough. I could barely speak Spanish, so even paying my bills was a frustrating process that left me in tears. I was reliant on camming for making money and my life management skills were not very good. I was scraping by and had to ask my mom for money a few times to float me to my next paycheck.

After only 2 whole months I made the decision to end my dream of living there. I was back on the permaculture farm and playing in the river with some of the local kids and the other farm worker who was volunteering with me, and all the kids wanted to jump off this cliff. There were 2 cliffs, one twice as high as the other. All the kids jumped off the biggest, no problem, but I decided to start with the smaller one.

When I hit the water, I sank down harder than I thought I would, and my feet made forceful contact with the dirt beneath the water below. Still, I went back up to attempt the higher one. As I was standing up there hearing the kids chant my name to encourage me to jump, I couldn't do it. I was worried because I'd sunk so deep on the first one that if I jumped off this one, I could potentially break a leg or get hurt. I was doing the mental math in my head, 3 hours from the city, who knows how far from a hospital, and my only contact a 68-year-old man who didn't have the word "urgent" in his vocabulary. Could I really take this risk? If I didn't jump at worst the kids would maybe laugh and be disappointed.

Maybe this isn't my cliff to jump, I thought. Maybe experiencing the smaller one was enough. Maybe Panama wasn't the big jump I needed to make right now, maybe it was the little one to prepare me for what's next. I realized that I had a choice. Embarrassment or feeling like a failure wasn't that big of a deal. No one could take away what I'd experienced, and I'd done it. Even if it didn't end the way I thought, I'd done what I had wanted to do. I lived in Panama, and I got to know my grandmother's country. Though I was never able to get to see her, I felt the spirit of my ancestors, the divine mother, and the breathtaking beauty of Panama deep within my heart.

Luckily there was no penalty for giving up my apartment early. I will cherish my time there and the almost yearlong adventure of going back and forth to try and achieve it, but in the end, I didn't stay friends with any of the people I met there. They didn't pursue any kind of connection with me. Since I was leaving the country that made sense. I still felt like the odd one out, a novelty pretending to be square, a lost dog looking for someone to feed and love her, still looking for her forever home.

***

I went back to Washington but could not bear staying with my mom again, realizing I needed to act like an adult. One of my friends from the industry had moved to Tacoma, WA and was raving about the cuteness of the Stadium district and still affordable apartment rent prices. She was correct.

Stadium district was named for the large stadium football of the high school made famous by Heath Ledger's singing in the movie *10 Things I Hate About You*. Stadium High School is an architectural masterpiece like something out of a fantasy story. The city of Tacoma has a somewhat dark and storied past but remnants of old-world charm, historical buildings and mansions are still scattered throughout it.

This was a temporary transition home for me while I figured out what I was doing with my life. It felt so good to have a friend from the industry living close by where we could talk about work, trade info and resources, and laugh about the absurdity of our days in LA. You could usually find us having cocktails by the water and going on walks with her little dog by the beach when we were not locked away inside hustling money from a computer screen.

It was idyllic, it was beautiful, simple, peaceful, but far away adventures were still calling me. This couldn't be it, the end of my story? There was something out there still calling me and not having any anchors or responsibilities holding me in place, I was more than happy and excited to answer the call.

And wouldn't you know it? Margot had invited me to come see her in Lausanne, Switzerland. It had been a few years since me and my ex-boyfriend had visited her and her new husband while they were living in Ibiza. It felt like the years prior to and during her marriage she was so busy with life we hadn't talked much so I was really looking forward to going to visit her and having a chance to reconnect.

It's funny how fate works.

Swiss Miss

Sweden?

No, Switzerland!

Why Switzerland?

Why everyone seems to confuse Switzerland with Sweden is something I'll never understand but I can tell you, Switzerland was never a why, but a who, which turned into a dream, and lasted due to an incredible amount of stubbornness.

Living back in Washington and in my new apartment I had no real direction, but I had a lot of drive. Literally, I was driving all over the place, visiting my mom in Roseburg Oregon, driving to LA, sometimes over to Arizona and then back up again. Thousands of miles and hours on the road, scraping by through scenes, camming, modeling, and whatever else odd jobs I could find. When I'd return home to Tacoma, I'd enjoy my time off by getting day drunk with my friend turned neighbor.

When people look at my life from the outside they see someone who is smiling, traveling, always bouncing from one place to the next. They've told me that they love to watch my life through my social media posts. It's easy to be bold and spontaneous when you have no real direction in your life, it's quite a feeling being so free, but the reason I'm always traveling is I have to go where I'm able to make money. I would get burnt out on camming, so I would plan a trip to LA. I make a couple thousand there and I try to visit my family because I've been gone for a month or two. I'd have an unexpected bill, so I put out a call for customs or photoshoots.

Then and now, I struggle with being proactive when it comes to my personal finances. It could be that I don't really love it anymore. At some point it all just became a job. There are good days, there are horrible days, but there are no paid sick days or vacation. I work, or I can't live. There's no such thing as a payday advance or loan as a freelancer. I make just over the margin to qualify for social services. That's the reality for most of us. I could cry about it, and I have, but tears don't pay bills.

Traveling became the way that I coped with the isolation this job brings with it. It made the physically hard days, emotional burnout, and social isolation more bearable. Just work my ass off for a few weeks or months, and then I could go play in Europe, or visit friends and family. At the time this balance suited me just fine and while I wasn't living a life of luxury, I learned how to stretch my money.

I went back to Switzerland sometime in late 2016 to visit Margot, who was now single and living with some friends. We would all smoke splifs, enjoy hikes in the gorgeous Swiss Alps and occasionally snort the longest lines of cocaine I have ever seen in my life. This was some Scarface shit, but no, not Scarface, Swiss.

Swiss people live in a little bubble of prosperity and safety. If you're not a gypsy and pay all your bills and taxes on time you can live a very nice life. Swiss people are traditionally quite conservative. The country is known for international banking, Nestle and Rolex watches, as well as being home to a ridiculously large number or multimillionaires. The government uses that money to benefit the people living there creating a safe, clean, efficient, and beautiful country.

I thought I could be a part of this bubble, even if just for a month here and a month there at a time. Maybe the glitz and glamour would somehow rub off on me, and I'd become a sophisticated lady eventually. When I spoke of my idea of renting a room from Margot and her 2 roommates in their new house where they were soon moving, I was met with exuberant enthusiasm. I was already traveling to Europe multiple months of the year, why not have a home base in Switzerland?

For a while it seemed like the plan was set and everyone was on board. The man, Paul, began looking for a house for all of us to live in and set his eyes on a tiny little village called Chevilly. The second roommate dropped out sometime during the process. Paul and Margot would send me pictures and updates while I was back in Tacoma, and it seemed like no time at all before I was crossing the pond again and getting to see the new house in real life.

The house was definitely spacious, but the town was drying up. The school had been closed for years and when we went exploring in the chapel, we were greeted by thousands of dead flies covering every surface of the inside of the church. It was definitely an omen.

During my first months in the new house, I started noticing some odd behavior coming from Paul towards Margot. When he came home, he treated her almost like a wife. If his day was bad, he would complain to her and though I didn't speak French at the time his energy seemed to become hostile towards her.

He was taking out his frustrations onto her almost nightly and at some point, I had to acknowledge what I was seeing and ask if I was wrong in my assumptions because I didn't speak French. Maybe this was normal for them? I talked to them both and they agreed that this wasn't kind behavior and Paul promised to work on not making his personal stress Margot's complete responsibility.

Then he forgot and the aggression in his voice became even more unpleasant. It was like being around two parents who were fighting but you had no clue what they were fighting about. We were all addicts of various sorts. Mine being weed and tobacco, some wine here and there, but Paul had a coke habit which didn't help the situation. He began using little gifts of weed as a way to get favor from me, and sadly it worked. I'm not really good at saying no to weed, but the unspoken fact was it was a bribe, for my compliance and silence in the toxic behavior.

Chevilly only had one or two buses each day, so it was really complicated for me to leave the house without a car. There was no grocery store in town, only a cheese vending machine, a very Swiss thing. Both Margot and Paul worked day jobs and had cars, so I was left on my own often and found weed to be a good friend.

As the holidays approached things in the house became even more tense between them. He was in love with her and had been for a very long time. It was unrequited and it finally came to a point that she could no longer deny that this relationship was extremely unhealthy. She and I had planned a trip to visit her family in France and by the time it arrived things had hit critical levels. We were happy to escape.

I love road trips with Margot, eating out and going on hikes, we could spend hours together without ever getting bored with each other. Maybe annoyed a little, but even that was part of the fun. Margot was a free spirit, and she made me feel like I could be one too. And our new addition that she had kept from the divorce, who came with us everywhere, was the softest and happiest little dog named Ficelle. Which means string in French.

Périgueux is east of Bordeaux, and it's known for growing black truffles, walnuts, and breeding ducks to make foie gras. It's a medieval area full of castles, ancient history in every corner and the region is part of the Vézère Valley, which is home to the famous 17,000-year-old Lascaux cave paintings. You can feel a sense of magic in the air. Or maybe that's just how it felt because Margot was so good at telling me all the stories and esoteric knowledge she could recall as we travelled through it together.

A French style Christmas is for experienced eaters only. If you can't handle the fat, get out of the country. Escargot smothered in butter and parsley and garlic. Duck, smoked salmon, countless baguettes, more duck… then a cake for dessert, and would you believe, cheese after cake for the final dessert not to mention all the chocolates and treats we'd nibble throughout the day.

Her family was intelligent, irreverent, board game enthusiasts, who loved to laugh, eat, and discuss many subjects of life. I remember feeling a lot of guilt at the time because I had been seeing less and less of my family now spending so much time overseas. Margot's sister gave me some of the best advice for guilt.

Do you think when you're gone their lives just stop? Do you think that they don't have fun, eat, sleep, and go about their days regardless of if you're there or not? This guilt you're feeling is ego. The ego saying without me they can't thrive, their happiness depends on my presence. Which, of course, sounded ridiculous. We were all living our own lives, and I was using guilt as a blockade from truly embracing living my own.

On the 6-hour drive back to Switzerland, Margot and I talked deeply, and we agreed the situation with Paul was unsustainable. Once we were back home, slightly delirious from the drive, family time, and late hour of the night, it was like a sign from God when we unexpectedly found one of the bribe nuggets of weed. Neither of us had been accepting these "gifts" from Paul before we left as we had figured out the cost attached to them. But that night we smoked, and we laughed until we cried.

We came up with 2 plans.

The first was the burger beret. The perfect combination of American and French culture (and so fun to say in a French accent). A Parisian style beret, but it's a burger design, customizable with your choice of whole wheat or sesame seed bun, meat, tomato, and removable lettuce. I know, genius.

The second was that we would get an apartment together and I would come for 3 months at a time (the max for a tourist visa) until I could figure out how to make the move permanently. I loved her, and she loved me, and we needed that love, that deep friendship at this time of our lives, we wanted to make this dream work somehow and we were both young enough to believe it could happen.

Thank God we couldn't see the future, thank God we couldn't see the hardships, the struggles and painful growth this plan would bring with it. All we saw was the perfect 2-bedroom apartment in a city called Ecublens, and the bright hope of a new chapter of life. For both of us.

At the beginning of all this I had kept my apartment in Tacoma but had only signed a 6-month lease and at the end of it, I would pack most of my life into a tiny storage unit, and begin this new journey in Switzerland. I was so happy. Living with my best friend in one of the most beautiful countries in the world. I would travel to LA for 1 or 2 months at a time and sleep in the spare bedroom of Spiegler's apartment and work to save up some money. Then I'd spend about 1 month visiting family and friends, sleeping on couches and spare rooms, and then travel back to Switzerland, to just live. Camming and launching my OnlyFans to supplement my income.

It became my home. The US was work, and Switzerland was my happy place, Margot was my family. She had a beautiful group of friends who welcomed me, and we would have dinners which were always incredible as most of her friends were gourmet chefs. Our nights out were so unique, and I loved the way they lived over there. I finally felt like I had a life. A normal life, with people I didn't have to hide my job from, and activities a normal mid-twenty something would do. We went camping, dancing at the club, hiking in the Alps. I had purpose in a way, and eventually I even started dating one of the friends in the group.

"You know all the guys would talk about how hot you were and how they wanted to fuck you, but I was never attracted to you." Said my now boyfriend, which I interpreted at the time to be sweet… I guess? I think that's a form of negging, but I was used to overt emotional abuse. It was easy to recognize bad behavior when two people were screaming at each other, but this man would be my next painful lesson.

Harry was a hardworking, and seemingly kind and generous man, that's what drew me to him. He was constantly busy or doing something for someone, as if relaxing was impossible. He was born in Switzerland and seemed to be cursed with the same productivity addiction as many other Swiss people.

I saw this as proof of his kindness and good nature, and we both loved smoking splifs, a mixture of weed and tobacco. He brought me into his life, and I enjoyed being his girlfriend and experiencing another side of the Swiss life independent of Margot. But there were so many cracks, so many red flags that I was too naive to recognize at the time.

The first time we had sex, he came inside me, the look on his face being one of shock and surprise. I wasn't at a point in my cycle where I was worried about becoming pregnant and just assumed he was very excited because it was our first time. But quickly I realized this wasn't a one-time thing.

He was a premature ejaculator, which in itself wasn't the worst thing, but I told him I couldn't be on birth control and would ask him every time to please wear a condom. He would fight me, or say let's start without one, only to end with the surprised shocked look on his face as he *accidentally* came inside me again.

How he could be surprised at this point was beyond me. This was what happened almost every time, and I grew more and more anxious and resentful for the stress this was causing me. I began not wanting to have sex because I knew the pattern now, and waking up in the morning to his hard dick painfully pressed into my back was giving me PTSD.

Did he not care about my feelings? My desires? My body autonomy? To the rest of the world he was so understanding and kind so my brain couldn't understand why I didn't get the same respect or understanding. I thought I was in love with him, but I can see now it was a trauma bond.

One night we were sitting in the kitchen, and I had made it clear I was looking for affection, not sex that night and he was not happy with this but played it off.

"Well, I could just pay you" he said with a laugh. It was such a strange moment. I tried to smooth it over wanting to believe it was indeed meant as a joke, but my body revolted. I heard ringing in my ears, and my heart was pounding, I couldn't catch my breath and sank down to the floor so I wouldn't pass out. His comment had triggered a panic attack in my body. My mind was racing trying to think of the right thing to say but my heart was broken how someone could be so callous.

My *no* didn't matter, my wants and desires for control of my body ignored. Some might disagree with this statement but knowingly putting someone at risk, not listening to their needs of safety, and coercing them into doing something they don't want to do, is a form rape.

At the time I didn't see that, but I saw the dysfunction, I saw the way my mental health was suffering, my life revolving around him and our never-ending dramas. I blamed myself, I blamed my weed habit, I began to try to regulate myself so much so I wouldn't get upset over "small things."

Like when he had another girl sleep in his bed when I wasn't there, and finding out when she climbed in his bed to retrieve her pajamas which were neatly folded and tucked under the pillow where I normally slept. Nothing happened, he said! Which I believed, but I tried to explain why this was disrespectful to me and our relationship. "It's not a big deal!" he told me as I continued to explain why I would prefer if he slept on the couch if he wanted to offer his bed to another woman. Or when we went to a party where I didn't know anyone and I asked him to hang out with me after hours of being alone, because I was feeling really out of place and my French was no good at this time, but he disappeared the rest of the night and then got pouty when I wanted to go home with Margot instead of him.

At that party one of his friends had called me a slag, and I was feeling so angry and ashamed and alone. I felt ugly and unwanted. It reminded me that I was still a novelty, the porn star, the whore, and still lacking the confidence needed to stand up for myself. I wanted to fit in, feel normal, prove that I was just like them, be cool.

But I felt so insecure.

Surprising to no one, after about a year, I became pregnant. The anger I felt is indescribable, the betrayal of my own body as my boobs got sore and swollen, fatigue like I'd never had before, my emotions all over the place. I was back in the US when I found out. That phone call could have been heard from blocks around.

I told you this would happen! We are not ready for a child; we can't even go a few weeks without fighting!

And the saddest part, the part that broke me the deepest… I wanted to have a baby. I wanted the dream of him and I, to be a happy family, for everything to work out, our Swiss happy ending. I wanted to be a mother so much, but I could never see myself tied to this man for a lifetime. I would kill myself, surely, if I had to put up with him and a baby.

So, I scheduled my very first abortion. I got a hotel room for 2 nights, and I took the pills that would start the process of releasing the little mass of cells forming inside me. I was around 7 weeks, and it was incredibly painful when my body gave birth to what could have been my baby. I felt so defeated, and angry, and so fucking stupid.

Sometime after, I remember having to shoot custom videos for my only fans, my breasts still enlarged as my body adjusted back to its state before the pregnancy. No one tells you how long it takes for your body to feel normal again. Would they know when they saw the video? Could they see my shame?

No. They just saw a hot girl with big tits. Which to be fair, is what they were paying for and being forced to not work the past months due to stress and the recovery time, I really needed the money.

When I went back to Switzerland months later, I had agreed to see Harry at the Cully jazz festival, and he was on his sweetest most apologetic behavior. He voiced to me his regret and understanding about how he had treated me and made promises to me that he would change, he'd seen the light. After a few glasses of wine, I believed him.

He lied.

The same problems were there, the trauma bond now even deeper and the escapism through weed now a necessity instead of pleasure. I was delusional, I thought this was real love because no matter how many times I said I was done, I'd come back to him apologizing for being so crazy, blaming myself for my unstable moods. Looking back, I think the relationship was so hard to leave because I had nothing that I was truly passionate about.

My only real-life goal was to get a visa for Switzerland and that was proving harder and harder. I had no job prospects outside of porn, and still often felt very lonely and out of place. I knew we were toxic as a couple, but at least I didn't feel so alone. And the good was good, the laughter we shared seemed genuine.

Soon, something miraculous would happen. I met Simone. First the night of the Cully jazz festival, we had all exchanged small talk at the chai tea stand. And then a few days later as I was walking on the street with Harry, one of our good days, Simone would drive right by us in her travel van she lived out of. It was sunset and she was bathed in golden light.

"Well, this is a sign", she said. "Here, take my card. I think we are meant to know each other."

A short while later she texted me and told me about a training she was putting together. A yoga doula. A doula is a non-medical woman's companion during conception, pregnancy, and postpartum and a Yoga Doula does this with the use of Yoga and kundalini yogic lifestyle practices. It was over $4000 USD and a total of 9 months, meeting one weekend a month for 2 nights and 3 days per weekend in the country's capital of Bern.

I'd never thought about being a doula, and my only experience with pregnancy was my recent abortion, and yet, I felt absolutely called to do this training. I had no idea how I would afford it, but they allowed me to do a payment plan and within a few months I was sitting in a yoga studio with 15 other women and we began discussing what it means to be a woman and to be in relation with the masculine.

The first weekend there were a lot of tears. Harry was helping a friend with his business in a nearby town called Fribourg and when I came home after the training the fights felt even more painful and lonely. His coldness, his ability to completely ignore me while seemingly also saying he loves me after hearing all day about examples of healthy and loving relationships during my class was a cold reality check.

This was waking up parts of my psyche I'd never visited, it was bringing to the surface generational trauma and pain I'd endured and highlighting my disconnection from this man who I also professed to love. It didn't feel like love, but I wanted it so desperately to, I wanted to fit in with the other women and their happy relationships, yet I also wanted to be spiritual and grounded in my truth.

By day 3 of the first weekend, I'd been crying for what felt like a solid 24 hours. I had Ficelle with me because I'd promised to watch her that weekend and it happened to coincide with the training. I had to pull over because the sobs were making it too hard to drive safely. A good Samaritan walking by stopped and asked through the window if I was ok. I said yes, thank you, and realized how insane I must look and pulled myself back together.

The emotional agony, the waterfall of hurts unleashed, the things I never spoke aloud were all now screaming at me. In the morning on the third day of the first weekend I texted Simone and said, it's too much. I would join the next round of training when I was more stable financially and emotionally. She gently encouraged me to come, that they would support me.

Walking through those doors I was so embarrassed, so ashamed of my inability to control my emotions, even feeling like somehow this must be an act, it must be that I'm just attention seeking, but the tears and the sobs shaking my body would not let me go. All the women sat surrounding me in a circle and had me lay in the middle as they sang songs and held their hands over me and each gave me a blessing. The matron, an original follower of yogi Bajan, gave me the blessing of dignity. Part of me resented that.

I don't have dignity because I'm a sex worker? Is that it? But I was in no position to show any rejection of her blessing as I was still laying in the middle of them all, feeling loved, supported and completely uncomfortable all at once. They let me cry, they let me feel, they didn't ask why, they witnessed my grief and sorrow and held me energetically through the waves as they grew smaller and smaller.

Never had felt this kind of support, and never from this many women. Women tend to dislike me, the porn star, the harlot, the liability that could take their man away at any moment. But there was none of that at this moment. This training was the true embodiment of women supporting other women.

9 months later I would finish the training, and during that time I would hold others as they faced their pain, I would witness the grief we all collectively carried, the pain of being a conscious woman, mothers, in this dysfunctional world. We would also laugh, our burdens growing lighter and lighter each weekend we shared together. There is magic in women supporting women.

This training not only gave me the knowledge of pregnancy, of the divinity and power of the female body, the skills to use yoga and yogic lifestyle practices to live a happier and healthier life, but it also gave me my power back. Real power, not from adoring fans, not from my beauty or sexual prowess, but from the deep inner well that's always been inside me.

My dignity was never tied to my job, it was tied to the horrible thoughts I kept on loop in my head. The most common being, you're such a piece of shit. The way I'd been speaking to myself and treating myself wasn't dignified, it was abusive, mean, and I would never in a million years speak to someone the way I had gotten used to speaking to myself.

The training ended February 2019, only a few weeks before the world would shut down and we would all learn what Covid was. Harry and I had been planning to get married, because our constant fighting and breaking up and getting back together was a clear sign we must really love each other, and marriage would allow me to stay in the country thus solving all our relational problems. Those plans got put on hold, thank God.

Due to this moment of pause I was able to seek the counsel of a specialist for people with BPD, which is what I thought I had at this point. When I explained the situation, how he ignored me when I pleaded for clarity or reassurance, the things he'd say to me, his apathy of my pain, and my reaction to all of it, she said it sounds like he is a narcissist. That word gets a lot of attention in our culture today and I had never gone down that rabbit hole myself.

This wasn't a formal diagnosis but an opinion from her professional experience and what I'd told her. This was the first wakeup call where I actually realized, maybe he wasn't such a nice guy. Maybe I wasn't as crazy as I'd been trying to make myself believe. Still, I bought a workbook for BPD and as I filled out chapter to chapter it became clear a lot of the information was not really reflective of my life as a whole. Sure, in my youth I had struggled a lot, but through porn, life experience and therapy those symptoms were not my daily or even yearly experience and as time had gone on I'd learned better coping strategies. I'd had healthy relationships. I'd been terribly hurt and not blown up someone's phone with 50 thousand texts or angry messages. I'd faced defeat, rejection, and heartache without ever losing my shit.

The insane behavior that I thought was BPD only showed up in its extreme after months and months of having my boundaries and emotions trampled on and minimized. I was indeed acting crazy, but it was the result of being emotionally abused and gaslit for years and taking all the blame onto myself.

I was angry. And it was valid. But I was directing it in the wrong direction.

The last phone call I had with Harry showed me just how little he actually cared, and with the new information I had, his cold and uncaring attitude when I was trying to tell him why his behavior was hurtful showed me truly what kind of person I was dealing with. I don't think he ever liked me. I mean he literally said as much during our first days together. He never liked me, but he liked the status I gave him with his male friends.

He didn't wear condoms because he didn't care if I got pregnant or not, my wishes didn't matter to him, and it was always about his pleasure and needs, over mine. Was he a narcissist? I'm learning that it really doesn't matter, my lived experience does. I blocked his number and got on with the healing that would be needed to close this chapter of my life.

***

Healing can come in many forms. It can be physical like getting your diet on track, or it can be environmental like changing your surroundings or social life to better align with your values, and it can be mental and emotional like doing therapy, but there's a part of healing that many of us don't consider or even value nowadays which is healing the spirit. I've always had a connection with God, and my darkest moments have usually been a result of a disconnection from that source, from divine love. The yoga doula training woke that part of me up again.

With all the politics around Christianity and religions and the pain that those institutions have caused people for thousands of years I tend to be hesitant to open up about this relationship I have with God. It's hard for me to even write the word God because I know it can trigger and lose people because of the baggage it's gathered. But for me, God is just love, God is miracles that can't be explained, it's the serendipitous moments and being in the right place at the right time, it's a frequency, and most importantly it's faith in something greater than myself.

There was a commercial back in the day for a credit card company, and the premise was a girl calling customer support and being treated with kindness and realizing it was actually her on the other end. The tag line: We treat you the way you treat you. I think that's the best metaphor for God and manifestation that I've ever heard. You want to be miserable and unhappy? God will give you every chance to change course, but true unconditional love means ultimately letting you choose how you live your own life. I believe, that because I felt like a piece of shit, I stayed in situations that enforced that belief. God is the force that put Simone and me at the exact same place at 2 separate times, God is the voice that said look to your left and let me see her driving down the street, and God is the energy that asked her to invite me to the training. I choose to believe that. You don't have to.

But what about war? What about famine and all the atrocities in the world?

I hear you. And to that I would say, humans kill humans. Humans start wars, because of greed and power and control, and humans are the only ones that can stop it. It's not God deciding who lives and dies, it's individuals. God is the moment of peace between the screaming matches, the tiny quiet flutter of hope in your heart when you are about to give up. God, the entity not the religion, is in every living thing. We can tap into that energy anytime if we just reach out and choose to, and sometimes God is there but we are so focused on what we don't have we can't see all the blessings that we do have.

Freewill means that you can choose to look at disheveled kittens you find on the street and think, gross they are dirty and have fleas, or you can look at kittens and think what precious beings, how can I help them? That's the energy of a loving god consciousness. You get to choose how you frame your world, but God is always there, God is inside you and every living thing. Even so-called narcissists.

I had forgotten and neglected my spirit, serving this man and all these external forces while allowing myself to be abused and participating in that abuse. Starving myself because I didn't feel worthy to have weight, to not look like some ideal fantasy, constantly doubting my own instincts and gaslighting myself into being a monster because it was easier than letting go of people and environments who were mistreating me. A direct reflection in my lack of connection, faith, and worthiness. Harry was a harsh wake up call.

The road to true self-acceptance would take another few years, but my connection to spirit was reignited in this moment. The flash of clarity started small, and it didn't feel great or life changing in the moment. I felt alone, broken, defeated, confused, and lost. Covid was just beginning and none of us knew what was happening, I wasn't the only one having to sit and wait, but I tend to get bored very easily and without the distraction of other energies pulling me in different direction I finally was able to listen to my own soul, and gently move towards my authentic desires.

***

Stuck again in a small room of my mother's house, who was now living in an eastern Washington city called Walla Walla, none of us knew when the world would open up again. For the first few months I continued to pay Margot my half the rent, but I was often late, and this was causing a lot of stress and uncertainty for her, understandably, so we agreed she should find a roommate until life went back to normal.

My mom and I have a loving yet sometimes complicated relationship. I credit her for my love of nature, cooking, natural healing, and going on little adventures. My past childhood hurts still weighed heavy on my heart, but my love for her has always been greater than any resentment. She's an over giver, making it clear that her love for my sister and I was unconditional, yet fearing that we might one day abandon her. Even though I could get triggered and feel like a kid when those past pains would surface, we managed to get through them and reach at the very least neutral ground which ultimately made us see each other more fully and authentically.

For the first time in my life, I started really focusing on my OnlyFans, consistently posting and responding to messages. I also had a web series come out and while I didn't feel like I had all the resources I needed to be my best, I managed to show up for the things asked of me. It was hard managing the stress of isolation, living with my mom, and being asked to show up on camera like the superstar that was expected, but one by one I got through each commitment, each task, and gained a bit more self-esteem as I completed them.

Better is the enemy of good.

Anything we do can always be better, it can always be improved upon in some way, but getting caught up in that is a form of perfectionism, and you know what's worse than better, or good, or even ok? Not finishing the damn thing and never making changes. Action is the only thing that can create change, that can give the lessons needed to grow.

For so long I felt like I was in limbo, not moving forward, not getting my basic life tasks accomplished, not taking care of myself, not knowing who I was or where I was going. Living in Switzerland was a dream come true but the cost was having to leave every 3 months, paying $1000 rent on an apartment I couldn't stay in 6 months out of the year, not to mention the cost of flights there and back, and the agonizing uncertainty of not knowing if I would ever be able to get a visa.

Many people tried to help, and each time I got my hopes up we would discover that the plan wouldn't work for my particular situation. The stress was taking a physical and emotional toll on me, but I didn't want to give up and I didn't want to disappoint Margot, so I tried to stay hopeful.

COVID was a reset for the world, and it was the beginning of me taking full responsibility for my shit because I had to. For me that looked like renting a hotel room every few weeks to shoot content, camming from my room for a few hours while my mom was at work, and spending a lot of time gardening and smoking weed in the backyard.

Though it was peaceful I got a little stir crazy and planned a camping trip towards the later part of the lockdown. Originally, I had wanted to go alone, solo camping was something I was enjoying during lockdown, but one of the producers of the web series I did asked if he could join me.

"So we can plan season 2?" I asked him.

"Sure" He responded.

Our relationship had healed somewhat after the series was finally released and we collectively breathed a sigh of relief since the nearly 3-year project was completed. It was not an easy process. I had to fight at every turn during pre-production, filming, and postproduction to be treated fairly. They almost hadn't cast me in the series after I had spent over a year and countless hours telling my stories from my work in the adult industry to this producer. He told me he never promised me the part, only heavily insinuated it.

Margot had warned me for giving so much of my time and energy for free with no written contract or agreement, but I believed in the project and wanted to help create something that was actually representative of our industry that didn't make us look like victims or idiots. At the end, I could only fight so much, the 2 other producers didn't want me in the show. Miraculously, with a very honest and vulnerable email I convinced them and a few weeks later I was on set filming the first scene.

Everything was down to the wire. No time for rehearsals because they waited so long to make a decision, choosing the male lead the day I got to town. Straight into filming, all dialogue was improvised, and I had to deal with 2 large egos who were constantly fighting for control. All the crew, the videographers, the stylist, everyone was laughing together, and we all felt the magic of what we were creating. The vibes were so good, except for the dick size contest that was going on behind the camera.

Eventually this culminated into a few incidents that not only made me feel unsafe but completely disrespected and the final days of shooting were tense to say the least. Being a professional I did my job and kept my attitude locked into what I needed to be doing. I also kept up my end of the deal and helped with the postproduction giving my opinion on the different edits.

I didn't talk to this producer in a friendly manner for months and he never fully took accountability for his part in the breakdown on set. This should have been a red flag for me, but I eventually forgave him, and we slowly started talking again. It was Covid I think we were all feeling more forgiving.

When he finally came out for the camping trip it all started well enough and there were even some moments of deeper understanding on my end for his specific limitations and the expectations I had of him. Nature is good for that. Revealing the truth. Towards the end of the trip, I thought we were on the same page, but I still felt uneasy. He had made a comment when I tried to bring up season 2 that was a bit foreboding.

"Did you only want to talk about the series? I thought we were friends?"

"I thought half the reason you were coming on this trip with me was to talk about the second season?" I replied, noticing his accusing tone. I sensed some unresolved feelings.

The fact was, he approached me with this project, he was the one who said the character was created and inspired by me. He was a fan, and wanted me to be in the pilot which I declined because there was no pay. He asked me to sign my professional name on the grant proposal to get the money to create the full show. Yes we were friends, but this was firstly a business relationship, and it was clear he didn't have very good professional and personal boundaries. At the time, and through that experience, I learned the hard way about them too.

He would write me out of Season 2 but promised me, "Don't worry we'll still pay you for your consultation." So, I consulted, they paid me, and we never spoke again.

***

Covid went on for what felt like forever and it seemed like the world would never open back up. Margot had found a new roommate in Switzerland, and I had found some routine with my daily walks and backyard gardening. The peace was nice, but I don't think my body knew how to be at peace. I'd been living a life on the go since I turned 17, maybe I missed the chaos, maybe I was going through my own COVID psychosis, maybe I was actually depressed, but when I was ready to give up on it all I remembered that this dream, living in Switzerland would be mine to make.

I was not going to give up on it because of some stupid fucking virus. Eventually the world would open up again, and I was going to be ready when it did. So I kept my head to the grind, got in to therapy, worked on my business, focused on my health, and pretty soon I was back, the dream was back, reignited, and I was ready for my happy fucking ending.

Fairytale Romance

Was it all a dream? A nightmare? My prince was gone, I cast him away with evil words spouted out in anger and exhaustion, I felt no remorse, at least at first. Am I the wicked witch in this story? Was he the dragon in disguise, keeping me locked in a tower and not the knight in shining armor which I had so hoped? Maybe life is a lot more nuanced than fairytales have led us to believe, and I have wanted to believe in them since before I could even speak.

Wishing I had magic powers and could perform astonishing feats, instead many times as a child I would find myself sitting in my room crying because my life was completely and horribly, normal. Entering my thirties I often wondered if it was time to put away these fantasies, but it seems my delusions now are the same as they've always been.

My favorite roleplay when I was in 1st grade was to imagine I was in a sci-fi thriller and would end up either shot or wounded and my play companions (little boys) would save me. In adolescence, before bed I would imagine my own version of certain TV shows where the strong female lead would be captured, tortured and then the handsome male co-lead would save her. And of course, then they would "make love." I would imagine the same thing, night after night, the scenario would rarely change. I fucking loved it.

When someone's actions repeatedly don't match their words that's called manipulation and according to all the dating advice out there, any self-respecting human is supposed to value themselves enough to walk away, with grace preferably, though that can't always be guaranteed. Even after breaking up someone for the right reasons, it doesn't make the hurt any less or stop the spiral of dissecting all the different angles, questioning every action and response.

Why did it go wrong this time? My shame is triggered.

It's because of my job, how does a porn star fit into a family?

It's because of my trauma. I'm emotional and broken.

I'm over-experienced and inexperienced.

I'm too jaded for my age, too boring.

Too much this, too little that.

My guilt is activated quickly. I have no energy, funds, or desire to do the things I want to do because I've spent all my time obsessing about my relationships. I see all the ways I've been self-abandoning, letting my health and vitality fall to maintain this cool girl persona. Behind closed doors I'm beating myself up because…

winces

I wanted this person to pick me. Even if it's painful to be breadcrumbed and treated like a booty call, I put up with it because it's the only way I could be in their life. After the painful past relationships I thought he was different, I was sure this time it was different because I was different.

throws up.

That stupid voice in my head endlessly repeating itself, "Time to let go, time to move on." I, an expert at this, annoyingly brush the thought away and with it all the frustration I have simmering inside myself. All that therapy, all that work, all the built-up confidence just thrown in the fucking trash at the first glimmer of someone showing you attention.

How could you have been so stupid? How have you not learned your lesson yet?

After all, as you know this isn't my first time performing the role of the damsel lost in her own fairytale. It's said that a little positive delusion about your partner can be impactful on the success of a long-term relationship but perhaps I'm a little too delusional. I don't ever take off my rose-colored sunglasses, they have to be forcibly ripped from my face. And in the aftermath, as I look at the shattered pieces, I am faced with the full spectrum of reality, which can feel very disorienting and shocking.

If I were to describe myself as a character in a fantasy novel, it would go something like this.

She projects a free spirited and effortless grace, a self-employed sexy boss bitch that makes great money and can do whatever the fuck she wants but in reality she's a jaded porn veteran who feels insecure most of the time and has the *potential* to make large amounts of money but often lacks the discipline, focus and energy to make it actually happen. Waving her flag of independence to the world, inside she's desperately hoping someone will come and enter her life and give her the support she needs, and the guidance to help her accomplish her goals.

I know.

Don't say it.

(daddy issues)

Take this book for example. True to form, instead of writing a book that's informative and educational, writing something so profound that it will change the world, I'm having a pity party and wallowing in all my relationship fuck ups. I'm sad. My little dramatic sensitive heart is hurting and feeling really mad and frustrated. What you're reading now is my emotional climax about how hard it is to date for me, a person who's been in the porn industry all of her adult life, and how fucking confusing it is to be human and feel love and emotions, and how I've spent years unable to express myself.

I'm cumming all over your face with my feelings. For some of you this is your first facial. Breakups do that to you don't they? Not cum on your face. They show you where you're still raw and hurting. All the dreams you had to give up along the way.

Pussy Garden was supposed to be a fun and informative holistic gardening guide with plants and recipes that were good for your pussy. It was so me! Actually, it was so *us*. It was going to be a token of love to me from my new love, Jack. A project we were going to work on together. He had just graduated and had a degree which allowed for a great amount of knowledge of plants, and sustainable agriculture, and I love my pussy, a lot. I'm not high maintenance, but she is, and she gets whatever she wants.

I am a porn star after all. My pussy is my career.

Jack knew how to eat healthy, and everything he made me was so nutritious, exactly like how I enjoy eating. Green leafy veggies, gluten free grains, farm raised meats and cheeses, and all of it organic. Call me a snob, I don't fucking care. That's how I like to eat, and more importantly, that's how my pussy likes me to eat. We were both so happy and I loved the way Jack would take care of us, and yes, I mean sexually as well. I felt so happy, safe, respected, adored. Sometimes when we had sex, I swear I would be in another dimension. It was all so heavenly.

Being really interested in the medicinal use of herbs and plants Jack prided himself on everything in his gardens being edible. It made him so happy to point out each plant and tell me the use and way to consume it, pointing out the specific "pussy plants" as we dreamed together of all the projects we could do in the future.

We would drink lemon balm tea and go into the forest and look for endangered orchids, sometimes foraging for stinging nettles or wild edibles. Stinging nettles, as the name assumes, are very stingy! But the plant is so good for you and full of minerals. It tastes like the color green. Try it yourself! It's literally everywhere, but make sure you wear some gloves.

My memories of the first months of our relationship were tinted with a warm, golden, glowing sunset. People have told me that being with me is like being on vacation. And I pride myself in saying, *my life is a vacation*. Followed up by, *but also every day is a workday*. It's hard for me to tell the difference sometimes, work and pleasure. Maybe that's part of my problem, why I get lost in my own fantasies sometimes. I'm reminded at times, life is not like that for everyone, normal people have structure, routine, important work engagements. Not me, I'm the epitome of a free spirit, until I have to make money and then I'm a stressed-out workaholic.

It can be very hard for me not to be consumed by my daydreams. Life can just feel so amazing, and as someone who has been to very dark places, when life is good, I want to savor every second of it. I was finally back in Switzerland after being away for 1.5 years because of COVID to see if I could find a work opportunity and I was in full on celebration mode. The pandemic was over! Hope was on the horizon! No more masks! No more QR codes to do anything! The fear was dissipating, and humanity was finally returning to its full glory! Four weeks after my arrival in Switzerland I met him, Jack, and he too was "on vacation" just having graduated university and not yet employed professionally.

Our first dates were wonderful, he was so respectful and funny and kind, we could talk a lot and when I told him about my work in adult films he was at ease and politely inquisitive. Although, as time went on I became more and more uncomfortable with the way he would approach the subject of my work, almost as a novelty, or inside joke that only he laughed at. I've seen this change in my lovers time and again. My work is a delicate matter with intimate partners. They act like they don't care, but they fucking do. In one way or another, they do. Their insecurity leaks out one comment or passive aggressive joke at a time but by then we've had sex so I'm flying high on oxytocin and my own delusions and could make an excuse for anything.

Losing count of the times I took that familiar train ride to his home, a big house in the middle of the Swiss countryside, I remember vividly the feeling inside me, like agitated radioactive cockroaches, a mixture of joy and terror. With 5 roommates and a huge vegetable garden out back, a special herb and another plant garden in the front, the house was surrounded by fruit trees and had a patio with grapes growing on the ceiling. You could see mountains in every direction, rolling fields of farmland, and the most gorgeous sunsets. The house itself smelled deliciously of old wood and there was someone always cooking something in the kitchen.

Eating meals made with vegetables picked just meters away, having lazy days dictated by the sun, walking in the forest, foraging seasonal plants and drinking beer in the evenings with his roommates, fun young people that were half post punk and half nature loving hippies. The house itself felt full of creativity and care for the earth.

I let myself believe in a future with these people, this was a part of my fairy tale ending of living in Switzerland. I could see us in the future; canning jams in the autumn, and picking cherries in the spring, working on the garden and eventually producing enough to go commercial. I believed in their dream and wanted to help if I could, I wanted to be a part of it. Who cares if I couldn't actually talk to them, my French being poor at best at that time. It was my beautiful illusion, and now they were a part of it.

Everything was perfect (in my mind). Sure, after this visit I would have to go back to the US for a few months, but we could do it, Jack and I and our love story was meant to be, this was it! My happy fucking ending and I would be damned if I didn't make it work this time.

Not immediately finding work as I had hoped, plan B was always to go back home and save $15,000 to pay for a French school. That way I could receive a student visa and live in Switzerland for a year and learn French, buying myself a little time to get used to this new country before jumping into work. More expensive, but also more straightforward. For me, it was never a matter of if (though I tried to remain pragmatic) but always when.

I had been actively working to achieve this dream of living abroad for 4 years, and I told myself if I didn't save the money this time around, a change of direction would be needed. I absolutely refused to believe that I had gone through these 4 years of struggle and painful growth and isolation for this not to happen. It was my destiny. Every sign told me to just keep going. I knew that if I could just focus, I could do this. Soon I would have my student visa and live in Switzerland and have an amazing boyfriend and an amazing life!

Originally, I thought I'd need 3 months, but the whole process became closer to 5, and even then I was a few thousand short. Luckily my school was fine allowing me to pay the rest off once my visa was approved. All I could think about was the finish line. Work, eat, hike, sleep, and counseling twice a week. Jack and I were doing the long-distance thing but it was rocky from the start. I had found he was still active on the dating site where we had met, along with new photos from a shoot we had both done with his friends on the farm in Switzerland. That was the moment I should have ended things because that was the moment he showed me how much he valued me, and that was the moment I showed how much I valued myself.

Full steam ahead.

Annoyingly, I heard my therapist's voice in my head. I saw all the work we had done for the past months, and I knew there were red flags. During our sessions she had tasked me to write a "fucking manifesto" which is a letter of qualities I was looking for in a romantic partner as well as those I would not tolerate. Hard nos. Jack checked every box. Except two. He drank alcohol every day, a big trigger for me coming from a family of functional alcoholics, and he had no connection to his own spirituality or something greater, he was a pessimist.

Look, I don't need people to believe the same way I do but think about it. You have to believe a future is possible in order to create it, right? This isn't about "God" this is about being able to see, plan, take action and manifest your goals and dreams because you believe it is possible to do so even when it seems terrifying or impossible. To believe in yourself, in your personal worth and life purpose, that you are a creator of your life, not a victim of circumstance, that's a belief in something greater.

"But he checked every other box!" I told myself. "But you have a tendency to fall for unavailable unstable men." I countered with.

The logical thoughts tried to push through the waves of feel-good chemicals and bonding hormones, my own shame clawing at the corners of this perfect image. Sure, maybe I didn't think straight away, this guy is *the one*, but I thought, what a perfect match to the future I'm wanting to build! What a partner to build side by side with! We want the same things! Right? A farm. Land. A joy filled life. Friends around us. Loving family. Marriage to that special someone and a lifelong commitment with the maturity to always be able to talk about everything, sex, relationship, and feelings together. Someone to grow and evolve with. This could be him, no? He would plant me a pussy garden and we would write a book about it (and of course our love). Like, how romantic right? And use the money to buy a farm and host retreats for bettering the world! And everyone would be jealous of us because we were so in love! He didn't need to be perfect; we could figure ourselves out together.

Ok I totally thought
I could make him the one.
Or I could make myself fit into this
small constricting box called normal.
So he would see me as the one.

Admittedly, I have a kink for being held at arm's length. Make me work for it, daddy, I love the mind games. And he did, I worked hard, and oftentimes, it stung. Oh baby, yes. Reel me in with love and affection and when I feel happy and safe, push me away saying you're "not sure" or "confused". Well, now that makes two of us. But the fact was he wanted to have fun, party, drink beer, fuck, and play in the garden. Can I really fault him? I was so deep into the cool girl trope, so committed to the role. He got a hot, fun girlfriend he could show off and have sex with consistently without ever fully committing to, and I could keep trying to attain my unattainable dream, continuing to suffer quietly. Now, that's romantic.

The story of two star crossed lovers who in the end save each other.

In all fairness I have to ask myself, did I really love him? Or did I only love the fantasy I had of his potential? Even perhaps the suffering itself? That's how you show unconditional love, right? And that dream of us on a farm, his beautiful hair and body glimmering in the sun while tending his garden and his sweetness and friendly, open demeanor welcoming women to our retreats and gardening seminars. He was always so kind to strangers. And above all, that garden we would tend. Feeding us, bringing joy to our table, our workshops, providing life in exchange for love and care.

I wanted that fairytale, I convinced myself at the cost of everything that if I just tried a little harder, or communicated a little better, it would come true. He would change, because he would see that we were meant to be. And yes, I know how it sounds. Writing this I am very aware of my delusion, but at the time I couldn't escape. I was a princess lost in the forest, and he was going to be the woodsman to come and save me, and we would live happily ever after, and everything would be OK because we had each other, and I understood him.

The term "limerence" is becoming more and more known in the self-healing and dating advice circles on the internet. It's when you fall in love with a dream, not the actual person or the reality of the relationship. The idealized version in your mind gives you more satisfaction than actual time spent together. When we were together, I often felt uneasy, like, why is he treating me with such indifference, sometimes even disdain? Logical me said, "warning, sustainability of the situation is highly unlikely!" But then limerence kicks in and instead of seeing any red flags or having firm boundaries of what I will and will not tolerate, I create a preferred curated reality of the potential of the relationship, disregarding actual information that doesn't line up with that fantasy, and try to mold myself and the other to fit this narrative. Classic

CPTSD symptoms, it turns out. When the wires become too crossed and the fantasy and reality start to clash, cue a nervous system response.

Dysregulation. It feels like my heart is being squished and my insides are vibrating uncomfortably and my whole body feels like it's shaking. My thoughts become more paranoid and irritable, but at the same time I'm frozen. Like I have to keep smiling and act normal so my discomfort doesn't show but fearing everyone can tell. My thoughts are torturing me. *Why didn't I ask more questions, I'm so selfish. Why can't I just be happy, I'm too demanding. He thinks I'm overly emotional and crazy. Am I being too emotional? Maybe I am crazy. Why isn't he saying anything? He doesn't want to deal with me because I'm too needy. Too much.*

Really confusing trying to have conversations with depth and emotion and also being terrified of being rejected for showing depth and emotion. I literally pick partners who have not yet mastered emotional intelligence and then get upset when they can't have a serious conversation with me about our relationship. Like attracts like. Obviously, I don't consciously do this, I actually try really hard not to, but the pattern continues. It never starts that way, and actually in the beginning there's usually a lot of healthy dialogue between me and my partners.

Until you find "the thing." Or they find the "thing." The thing that's still sensitive, still raw, that phrase, or that look which brings you back to feeling powerless, or mistreated, humiliated, a child. The world moves in slow motion, a flash of reality cutting through the haziness of the dream. *Oh, no, I'm not safe*. I'm reduced to a trembling gerbil, watching a confused child poke me with a stick like he's not quite sure what to do but really just wishes I would go back to being cute and making adorable squeaky noises.

Dysregulation.

I wasn't sure what was happening for many years of my early adult life. I could manage mostly on my own with webinars and reading self-help books. When it would get really bad in the past or if I became worried for my own safety, I would seek the services of a therapist or coach. Enough to get back on track anywhere from 1-2 sessions up to 9 months and then continue "raw-dogging" it through life, as my friend calls it. I recently had to explain this phrase to someone. Rawdogging is a pretty vulgar term for fucking without a condom, meaning one who takes risks and goes out in the world with no protection. For the mental health metaphor, the dick is your mental health/neurodivergence and the condom represents using medication, having a therapist, and or a community so you have the best chance of health. For a very long time, I had no condom.

Luckily, I figured out a long time ago that all the cool kids go to therapy, and because of those numerous therapy sessions and the continued work in between, I have witnessed in myself growth, evolution, more maturity, and less stress. But there is a small child in me who screams sometimes *"Is it ever going to be enough?! When does self-work end?"*

Being single I'm more able to do the things I need to do to stay in a healthy mental space, but the balance gets off so quickly. One week I'm eating quinoa and dark leafy greens, the next I'm surviving on bread, cheese, and supermarket sandwiches. It's the dysregulation. It's the little vibration of anxiety, this low current just buzzing in the background waiting to grow and take over. Vitamins help. And sleep, and a balanced diet, and exercise, and water consumption, and limiting alcohol…

So fucking boring.

I often rebel against this conservative nature, but then my body rebels back and I immediately surrender. That's a war I don't want to win. My body is my best friend; we go everywhere together and have had so many fun adventures! I freaking love my body! I want to be its biggest supporter and ally because I've had years where my body was my enemy and I refuse to go back to that.

If my life is a garden, then I have some problems that need tending. I have some places that need extra attention, extra nutrients, extra love. I need to rip out some invasive species that have overgrown and are choking out the light. I need to populate the spaces with the right plants, the right balance, to create a dynamic ecosystem. I need to stop outsourcing my life and purpose to things, or people, outside of me.

It can be done, that's always been my belief.

Limerence is when you love someone and they in no way return those feelings of affection or even know you exist in some cases. But the sad truth, the thing that makes it so hard to move past, in my heart I believe we did have love and desire for each other. I don't think my expectations were unrealistic, and maybe even a part of him wanted the dream too but I would find out that he had been seeing and trying to rekindle the relationship with his ex-girlfriend the entirety of our relationship, which explains, well everything honestly. I'll never know all the details because he was never brave enough to tell me, I had to hear it from a friend. He would always say, "You want something from me that I can't give you."

But all I ever wanted was the truth. The one thing that was always in his power to give me.

If I had been an orchid he would have yelled at others for trampling on me, beaming with joy at finding this rare flower, he would have taken extra care to nurture and protect me and the environment I lived in. But I was a human being, and I made him feel small and inadequate. So, he took his insecurity on me. Hindsight is 20/20. He hasn't changed, maybe he never will. He will run from love and use women's bodies and hearts for validation until he finds the courage to face his greatest enemy. Himself. I was just collateral damage in a war that was never mine, but it would take me years to see that. At the time, I was devastated.

I thought this was my happy ending?

After that I had some self-esteem and confidence issues to work on as well as 6 months left on my student visa and time in Switzerland. I was effectively alone in a foreign country learning a new language, starting my social life from scratch while going to school and still maintaining my online adult work to survive. I think that's also why, even after he was gone, I grieved for him so much, grieved the dream.

***

When I arrived in Switzerland to begin that one year of schooling, everything in my life started to fall apart, everything I was sure about became unsure, the people I trusted were lost in their own lives and couldn't give me the support

I was seeking. It was one of the hardest life experiences I have ever been through. Every day since my arrival, I was living outside my comfort zone.

For the first 6 months I was sleeping on the couch because Margot wasn't comfortable letting go of her new roommate still anxious to be put in a financial hardship should my visa not be successful. When the roommate would sleep at his girlfriend's house I'd get to sleep in my old bed. But it didn't feel like mine anymore. It wasn't.

Depression and burnout had been kicking my ass, and I had to drag myself out of the mud over and over. Functional freeze is quite the bitch. Jack was supposed to have been my teammate, my partner, my hero, but life and reality, insisted otherwise.

I love Margot and feel closer with her than I've ever felt with another human. We can share things that are wrong, dark, unevolved, spiritual, frightening… I can be myself with her and that freedom is like honey on my soul.

Both of us have always been committed to our growth as healthy humans and spiritual people. We have a shared optimism of a beautiful future and find time to honor our present with countless adventures and travels, laughs and all-night dance parties. Margot is unlike any woman I have ever met and for a long time I thought we would grow old together, two little old ladies sitting on our porch of our farm being just as weird and irreverent as we are now.

My intuition told me things were different when I came back, our relationship didn't feel as in sync or as connected post COVID. We were both going through massive life transitions triggering all the intense emotions in each other. Knowing her so deeply it was as if no matter how hard I tried I couldn't detach, I couldn't *not* offer a listening ear, even when I was behind on my own work. And she couldn't help but worry about me, seeing my lack of action and lethargy in moving forward with my plans for staying here.

Both of us were escaping through the other. We tried counseling and it did help us get some clarity, we tried to work through our own feelings and insecurities, but my soul had been telling me for months that I needed to separate, to be independent. After the roommate moved out and I had my room back the house still felt foreign to me. I didn't feel welcome.

Margot was my lifeline, my anchor, my mother figure, and my social life. We loved being so close, but in that closeness, I was escaping through her, not actually creating my own life. I was a baby bird afraid to leave the nest which I had long outgrown, and tired of her overbearing energy constantly focusing on my success.

Neither of us wanted things to change, but they already had. We had begun fighting in a way we had never before. Her changing moods and erratic emotions were confusing to me, and I was resentful of having to be the emotional regulator. There was no room for my own emotions and I would end up smoking until I was catatonic to deal with them. This only furthered the problem.

Being 8 years older than me I always saw Margot as a big sister. I wanted to love her, impress her, take care of her and felt constantly judged for my slow progress and lack of motivation which then caused me to dink deeper into avoidance of my problems and furthered my lack of motivation.

Because we'd become so close, I couldn't exist fully in the space with her, the title of friend and confident, feeling more important than entrepreneur and student. For me there was no other option except a forced reset. Neither of us was dying, and I wasn't moving back to America tomorrow, simply into a different apartment. We talked about her ending the lease on our 2 bedroom a few months later and moving into her own 1-bedroom apartment. We found a young college student to take my room for the remaining months, and I would begin living in Airbnb's. It felt like my whole world was crashing, change was sweeping me away and all I wanted to do was desperately cling onto the hanging roots in the river. But everyday I'd put on a happy face and go to school and speak in French with my new classmates and do my best to acclimate to this new routine.

It's not easy trying to differentiate my intuition and trauma. What is coming from my soul and my heart and what is an attempt to escape things that make me uncomfortable? But staying in the places which trigger me feels worse. Is it dysregulation? Is it depression? Am I burnt out? Am I a narcissist wallowing in her own self-pity? Do I actually have some sense, but my own trauma gets in the way of seeing it? Am I overthinking again? All I know is when I feel that darkness pulling me down it scares me to be around people because I don't want to drag them down with me.

This adventure, this crazy dream of living in a foreign country for a year and learning a new language, was my responsibility alone. This was my time to learn how to save myself, and how it's messy and clumsy, and so fucking awkward, and how often you think about giving up. I wanted to just go home, to say, ah, I tried! But the other lesson was to finish what I started. My goal was to live in Switzerland for a full year and learn French and no matter what it takes, I was going to do that.

Turns out, I always had the power to act, and faith in my ability to do so, I just forgot.

My life is allowed to be magical and full of adventure and spontaneity, because that's how I've fucking designed it. And honestly it did take me being beaten down, witnessing the slow torturous death of my ego, the magnifying glass burning holes in all my coping habits and the crumbling of all my feeble crutches that I'd been clinging to forever. It was not a glamorous time. I needed to find my strength, my courage, and my faith, I needed to accept myself as the messy goblin angel baby I am. I needed to be mad, and sad at everyone and no one. At the end of it all, remember that I am my best friend. Literally til the end of time.

I'm still writing my fairytale one page at a time, now more conscious than ever of the words, the intentions and the direction that I am taking it. I learned I can be the knight, the heroine, the dragon, the queen and the fucking princess, as long as I don't forget the lovely little shining human that is Lacy. Returning back to myself over and over, feeling safe in my heart; I'm a big advocate for roleplay but I am an even bigger advocate for self-acceptance, self-love, self-worship, and finding home within one's own body. That is what I think we all deeply crave. Even porn stars.

But I wasn't quite out of the woods yet.

Demons

Spending so much time alone was a huge wake up call. Just because I can, doesn't mean I want to. I want friends. I want to develop close loving relationships with other humans that I can smell, see and hug. I fucking love people! I get along great with people and I make friends easily! Hiding from others is another form of self harm. I may not be smoking weed or drinking alcohol for the moment but I can say spending so many days alone and truly isolated I could feel the detrimental effects on my body. I could tell that if this continued it would make me physically sick.

Loneliness is an epidemic in our world, there are millions of people that feel this way often. That are isolated due to illness, or social status, or mental conditions or whatever the fucking reason. Loneliness makes you do and think crazy things and it drains your energy slowly but consistently.

Before I could believe that I was happy being alone, especially on my camping trips or my long drives from Seattle to California. I enjoyed the moments of solitude, but the end was always a loving friend waiting for me when I arrived with a hug and somewhere to sit, ready to listen to me share all my thoughts and funny stories, ready to connect with me through our shared loves. Life is about connection, this is more certain to me now than before. We need others. I need others.

And yet there I was, going on week 5 of living in hotels and Airbnbs completely unsure about where I'd stay next week, if I'd get a job to stay in Switzerland, trying to balance this new found wisdom and the very real need to make money to survive hoping that there are no emergencies that make my fragile house of cards come crashing down.

But somehow each week I would cam enough to afford the next Airbnb, I would distract myself by logging into my OnlyFans and shooting new content, I would go on long walks through the city I was in and I would soak up all the beauty of this foreign country. I wish I didn't need to be in psychological distress to be good at managing my business but it doesn't take away from the fact that I was managing, dare I say, thriving?

Still, there was so much doubt. It's like I needed the stress because it kept me moving. I'm scared to surrender and trust because trusting isn't always the thing that works out for me. I can't trust myself to trust the right things.

Will it all be worth it? At this point setting goals seems so hard to focus on, my only goal was to make it to the end of my student visa. Am I allowed to say that year was the most uncertain and insecure I've been in my entire life? That I absolutely hated the lack of knowing and comfort? I actually did quite well in my school, progressing each week and speaking more and more French. I forced myself to meet new people and create my own social life. Taking it day by day, I kept going.

Toxic positivity, manifesting, you are what you think, all these new age rules and warnings running through my head. That's the real trap, thinking I have to be happy all the time, or that if I'm sad sometimes there's something wrong with me.

There is nothing wrong with having emotions but I was dissecting every single one of them trying to make meaning and purpose out of them.

Why do I want to go back to an ex that couldn't even be kind to me? *Well, probably because that's the pattern I learned in childhood.*

What does that say about me? *That says I need to work on building my self esteem and learn what my boundaries are.*

Why do I think I deserve that? *I've lived my life pleasing others and I've taken on the responsibility of being perfect so when I do stand up for myself and get negative feedback I abandon my own needs instead of allowing other people to have their own emotional experience.*

Why am I not meditating even though I always feel better and more connected to my heart and soul? *I need to feel these feelings I've been holding back most of my life and not escape through my mind.*

Why am I eating cheese and processed carbs when I usually enjoy healthy foods and take joy in taking care of my body? *They taste good and I'm healthy and eating some carbs is better than starving myself.*

Why am I punishing myself? *That's what I was taught.*

And how can I stop? *Make the decision to.*

Simone said something in our doula training that has stayed with me to this day. She said, "Everything is serious, and nothing is serious."

So many things were going right, feeling success with my work and being brave pursuing activities that are healthy and sustainable with people who are healthy and sustainable. I started a friendship with a girl named Ellen and she's became such a kind and loving comfort during this time. She made me feel seen and understood, not victimized simply allowing me to be real with my feelings. We've remained friends since then and it's been so special to see how each of us has grown since this time.

Sometimes when I'm alone I dream of going back to the past, but which past? Never get into porn? Never meet Margot? Never get into a bad relationship? Even with the difficulties imagining these memories and moments being taken away is too painful. They've all given me so much, and maybe I'm selfish but I wouldn't trade the good to forget about the bad.

I can't go back. Sometimes you just need to be in limbo surfing the unknown and catching waves as they feel right. I don't know when the grief will end, but maybe I can allow myself to enjoy the waves? Enjoy the sun on my face, enjoy the feeling of the water on my skin. Be so fucking in the moment that I can't think of the possible shark swimming somewhere out there, because there are always sharks, jellyfish, or seaweed which is more gross and distracting than dangerous. It's all part of being in the ocean.

Can I surrender to being present with myself? Feeling complete in the moment. Exactly where I am. With or without friends. With or without certainty? Can I commit to finishing this book? Can I commit to exercising and meditating? Can I love myself the way that I would love my own child? Can I treat myself the way I wish for a romantic partner to treat me? Can I parent myself the way I wish my parents had? Can I stop self harming? For good?

One step at a time.

My school visa was finished in March but before that I celebrated Christmas and New Year's Eve and my birthday alone. This was both by choice and because I had no other appealing options. I had been invited to a dinner for people alone on Christmas, but I was terrified to go. No money and no way to afford a train ticket was also a factor. One of my friends Boris had taken us to the Christmas markets and helped me when I needed to move into yet another Airbnb. He helped me feel the Christmas spirit.

On Christmas Day however, I preferred to wallow in my own sadness. It was comforting to not have to put on a face or act like everything was ok. How exactly did I end up alone in an Airbnb eating pasta and cheese and watching too many hours of Netflix while the rest of the world was celebrating together? I was wondering the same.

I mean, hell, how did I even end up living in fucking Switzerland? It started innocently enough like all adventures do. Your standard run of the mill, haven't seen my European bestie for a long time and now that she's single again we finally get a chance to hang out and have some good ol' fashion girls time-visit.

My codependent tendencies were still hiding from my conscious awareness. It was hard at first to realize that I was codependent. I was just a nice person, right? But codependency is the need to be needed by another. This behavior was something that I recognized and resented when it was coming from my own mother but took years before I could see that I was exactly the same.

Our first years living together were full or joy, adventures, parties, and dinners with friends. We called each other wife but had decided that we were not actually romantically attracted to each other. It was a friendship and we would occasionally film scenes together but sexually we wanted different things. We were two different people who had lived independent lives.

Those differences became clear very quickly but we managed to talk through our disagreements and love each other for our uniqueness. We both came from our own background of childhood trauma and would have long talks unpacking our coping strategies and discussing why exactly we are the crazy girls we are.

During those years together I saw Margot struggling with working her nightshift as a nurse in a long-term care facility. Sometimes she would come home and be beaten down, literally and figuratively by the patients she had to deal with. It felt meaningful to be a friend in those moments, to give her a hug when she was sad. And when I was dealing with family struggles, being lost in my own life, feeling burnt out on my career as a sex worker, she was a caring and listening ear.

There was a moment when we were both faced with reality yet again that I may not be able to live in Switzerland full time and she asked me, are you doing this for you or are you doing this for me? At first, it was for her. I never thought I would be paying full time rent with her, I had just wanted to rent a room and be able to travel in Europe, but it changed over time. I committed to splitting the rent with her for our 2 bedroom, I committed to finding a way to live there and eventually my dream took on a life of its own.

I wanted Margot to be happy and safe but I realized that I also had to live my own life. Dating Harry, taking the yoga doula training, saving up money for school, then dating Jack, all of these experiences reinforced my commitment to living there. And still the duty of attaining a visa was my own.

Over our years together, I watched Margot completely change her life, becoming a sex therapist, finally quitting her job as a night nurse, feeling happier in her own life, but it was like I was still existing in the same plane I'd always been. The lost girl looking for her home. This became frustrating for both of us.

She expressed her concern over my lack of motivation, my over consumption of weed, my volatile relationships and my inability to follow through on various plans. She was right. And it made me feel even more like I was letting her and myself down. Still, I couldn't find the magic solution. I almost gave up during Covid and maybe I should have, yet I felt like I would have been giving up on her too. Just another thing that I don't follow through with.

I had to prove to her, and myself that this was my dream, that I wouldn't give up when things got hard, and I would try everything I could to make it happen. There was something inside me that said, you can't give up, you were so close before Covid, just try one more time.

It's easier for me to put my needs aside and focus on how I can help other people with their problems and be the caretaker or the nurturer, the mama or even daddy sometimes. Finally I felt like I was doing something for me. It may have started because of my delusion of being a hero but then it became everything to me, the thing that filled every waking thought I had, it drove me to work, to continue with my therapy. I thought that I was dealing with these blocks that were keeping me from claiming that life I dream of.

And maybe I was.

Therapy is hard, it's painful, it's ugly sometimes to face yourself. The ego gets in the way, your friends and family can get in the way, it feels like your entire world and identity crumble around you and leave your head spinning. Just a never-ending feeling of uncomfortableness. And trying not to escape? What a joke, the only goal is to actually even notice when you're escaping. I had an amazing coach and therapist during Covid and I was going twice a week. One day for my business coaching and one day for my mental health coaching. It was the structure I needed, they both helped me transition from struggling girl to sovereign woman. Fuck that's how I learned what the word sovereign even means. When I came back to Switzerland I was sure that things were going to be different this time.

But old habits, and toxic relationships, die hard.

Just because I knew the information, I hadn't practiced it yet and undoing patterns I'd been living my entire life wasn't an overnight thing. Upon arriving I was doing yoga everyday, I was eating healthy and following a spiritual practice, I felt beautiful inside and out. And slowly I saw all that energy fade, replaced again with uncertainty, weed, and unstable relationships.

My soul had started outgrowing this environment, I started to realize that I don't want to have to shrink to fit in with people and places. I had a different opinion and view of life than the people that I was around. But I was too fucking scared to own it so the only other option was to again shut those parts of myself down, try to fit in.

I stopped going to therapy a few months after I came back and the reason I told myself was that I couldn't afford it. Which was partly true, I wasn't working like I should. I was sleeping on a couch the first months, I was dating a guy that had already made it clear I wasn't a priority, I still wanted to be the cool girl, the fun easy going friend. My recent growth didn't match my surroundings and that conflicted internal feeling resulted in me staying frozen unable to take action.

I still didn't trust myself.

But I couldn't go back, or unlearn the work I'd put so much time, money and effort into learning. Eventually I had to listen to my needs, I had to make a fucking decision and choose my own wellbeing. Spending the holidays alone was a culmination of 2 years of therapy and boundary setting and it didn't feel joyful, celebratory, or like I've crossed some great personal milestone.

It felt like not tolerating people and environments that didn't support my health and growth would be a very lonely life. They may not be the deepest or most vulnerable relationships, but at least when you're cruising with all your fucked up friends you're not lonely, and you're never bored because cumulatively your lives are all shit shows and you depend too much on the opinions of others so it's all gossip, drama, and emotions and it feels glorious.

Being semi-forced to be alone for weeks during the holidays was really hard, facing myself in all my darkness was pitiful and depressing. Not to mention, I am a master escape artist and I still tried to escape though TV, social media, music, and long walks. My sadness is a friend, more so even than my spirituality. And my spirituality is quite shitty when I'm alone. Mediation feels like a chore and not a pleasure, yoga is torture, and I pray but usually when I'm begging for things to change. It was so frustrating to think how healthy my life felt before coming back, and easy to blame everyone around me, but I had to sit with my choices. I had to take responsibility.

In that loneliness, that period of having nowhere to go, being forced to face my demons, being forced to get a real clear picture of the state of my life and I'll be damned. I think it worked. At some point I just had to stop hating myself. I became tired of being tired, sad, and lonely. I realized behind all the torment and projections and internalized whorephobia that… I actually love who I am.

I could look in the mirror and see the new wrinkles on my face, the way my hair is turning gray, the newly acquired fat on my belly, the lingering heartbreak from my recent breakup, my social awkwardness, my imperfect eating and sleeping habits, even my desire to occasionally smoke and drink alcohol, and I could deeply in my soul love all of it.

Being human isn't a gift, it's a necessity because it is reality. By now you know I love a good fantasy, to get lost in a captivating romance, to dance with hope on one sleeve and a bleeding heart on the other, constantly escaping by vacillating between different worlds and dreamscapes.

Reality has warts, disaster, disease. People die and leave shockwaves of sadness behind them, really bad things happen to innocent people, evil triumphs too often and it seems like we are on a collision course for the apocalypse. Reality is war, famine, genocide, lying, cheating, scamming, people without homes, community or care.

And as fucked up as it is…reality is also dipping cookies in your tea and trying to eat them before they melt and fall to the bottom of your cup. Reality is also the flowers blooming in spring signaling the end of winter. Reality is also getting into a laughing fit with a friend thinking you may pee yourself yet unable to stop as tears stream down your face.

Reality for me was, though I have faced my trauma and "done the work" for many years, when push came to shove it was extremely hard for me to take care of myself in healthy consistent ways. Finally, there was no one else to blame, which in itself felt great. Taking full accountability was freeing and terrifying. I loved it and hated it.

Every demon I had been running away from, my sadness, my loneliness, my fears, my doubts, my anger, all the darkest parts of me which I was ashamed of were freed. Before, I would only allow them to come out for brief controlled moments and then quickly hide them away in a cloud of smoke.

Now they insisted on being seen. So, I watched movies with them. We laughed cynically together while eating our favorite foods and watching our favorite shows. We celebrated together when I was successful with my work and sometimes sadness and heavy despair would cuddle with me until I fell asleep. I began to see that my demons wanted to help me, they wanted to fight for me and with me.

The parts I thought were evil were actually just trying to love me. The anger I was so ashamed of wanted me to say fuck you to people who were unkind to me, not turn the other cheek and take the abuse. The grief and depression wanted me to actually feel the sadness that I had been avoiding so that I could finally let it go. The guilt and perfectionism wanted to watch scary movies and eat sweet treats if I wanted to because life is meant to be lived not feared. The loneliness wanted to show me how my maladapted ways of relating to others and gently encourage me to get out there and make real friends, loving friends, friends who see me for me. The stress and anxiety showed me how determined I am, how resilient I am, and also how soft and tender I am all at once. They looked at me, the full me, saw all my perceived faults and told me, I love you, just the way you are.

They whispered to me, "There is nothing to be ashamed of."

Maybe we all have the same demons. Deeply maybe we all are just awkwardly decaying adult bodies housing the remains of the frightened child within. Trying to comfort ourselves with anything that makes the emptiness go away. Can I fault myself for this path I've chosen? Can I actually say that even with this never-ending loneliness that I wouldn't do it again the same? The world is lonely. This career gave me life, wisdom, adventure, love, it gave me power. And that is what scares me. That is the mark of the exact pain point I have avoided over and over. Why do I freely give my power away, to men, to situations, to losses, even to the industry itself?

At 18 my energy was "pick me." Tell me I'm something amazing. Tell me I'm sexy. Confirm my worth. It felt so good to be rewarded with this lust and affirmation. Every box or magazine cover and every award nomination was a gold star to my ego, but that's what I needed then. I needed an identity, and I needed a strong one. And Lily LaBeau was strong, and sexy, and nasty, and she was so fun to be. I went years without hearing my real name, and I didn't mind. I didn't see my mom for 2 years. Barely noticed. I loved feeling like I belonged to something.

But eventually I didn't need that. It felt fake, shallow, hollow. I'd spent so long developing the brand that is Lily LaBeau that somewhere along the way I had lost sight of who I actually was. I was viewing myself through the lens of the fans, the directors, boyfriends, friends, everything outside of me. But who was I? Without Lily what did my life actually stand for, what actually brought me joy?

Being in nature, watching plants grow from seed, breathing the fresh morning air with a touch of coffee mixed in with it. Waking up to the sound of birds, learning a new hobby, feeling the creative gears in my head turning furiously when I'm swept away with inspiration. Gathering with women, singing together, sharing about life, love, hopes and dreams. That's what makes me feel alive.

But I'm supposed to be a sex goddess?! I'm supposed to be a kinky freak who wants to fuck everyone and is always down to be a slut. I'm supposed to love everything to do with sex. I'm supposed to not have an issue fucking random dudes for money.

Maybe as a porn star I'm supposed to be all those things. But I don't like people telling me what to do and I think it's time I decide for myself who I'm supposed to be instead of letting everyone else tell me. That year of living in Switzerland and all the years leading up to it, these demons, as well as some angels, set me on the path to finally choose who that person is. I realized that while I can be successful in chaos, I don't want to be. I want to put down roots, to stay in one place for more than a year, to build up my finances and make plans that will benefit my future.

Living in two different countries, traveling all over the world, learning a new language shaped me and gave me so much. I am thankful for these experiences and spending my twenties learning, growing, and making many, many mistakes, but I'm tired now. I want stability. I want a life that is consistent, supportive, and peaceful. I want to accept myself and take care of myself. I want to trust that others can do the same.

Eventually I did make it through the year of school and at the end I did not get an offer for a work visa though I applied to different sex worker friendly businesses. I helped Margot move out of our 2-bedroom apartment and into a new 1-bedroom place close to her work that was suited perfectly for her. She's working full time as a sex therapist, and she's booked out months in advance. After my schooling ended Ellen and I went on vacation to the south of France to celebrate the end of my time in Switzerland. Then I took all the memories and moments and my newly acquired French with me as I packed my bags and returned to the United States to begin my life over yet again.

To Be or Not To Be?

"I want her to die." I said with more bitterness and anger than I intended, my tone was low and hostile. "I'm so tired of meeting people and them only seeing her. She is a trauma response. She was created to keep me safe in an unsafe environment. I don't need or even want her anymore. I fucking hate her."

The silence on the other end was loud, both of us slightly astonished with the statements that had just come out of my mouth. Clearly, I was in a dark place surrounding my work and my new relationship and it wasn't the first time I had visited, but at this moment it felt so raw and close to the surface that even I was scared by my honesty. Do I really hate a part of myself? Is that even allowed? Spending so much time taking care of Lacy I hadn't realized that there were still issues in my relationship with Lily.

After coming home to Seattle from Switzerland in December of 2023, I had a vague idea of what I wanted to do with my life, along the lines of: make money and have fun but also be healthy. What I hadn't factored in was this vast feeling of emptiness and disorientation that I felt without this big dream of "MOVE TO SWITZERLAND!"

Now I had to really ask myself where am I going? What's next? And without this grand fantasy and goal it felt like all my passion for life and drive to action had vanished. I was simply existing.

Switzerland taught me so many things. How to stand on my own, understand my boundaries, face my darkest parts, and on the happier end of the spectrum it taught me how to engage in casual conversation with strangers (in another language mind you), make friends and push myself to engage in activities outside my comfort zone. I learned the importance of community and friendship and also that sometimes you need to reach out to others when you're in need of a hand. I was blessed by so many people in my time there, my classmates especially, and really found my flow with the culture and lifestyle.

Coming home and starting over again, acting "normal" as if this amazing life changing half decade of my life hadn't just blown me up and pieced me together into a whole new person felt so strange. As if I didn't want to tell everyone who would listen about every little miraculous moment and all the divine interventions and lessons I'd learned. Of course I did! But no one really seemed to care, caught up in their own lives.

And with enough demands to keep me occupied and depressed for the first few months upon arriving I didn't have the energy to push for more. It was time to finally answer the question. What the fuck am I doing with my life?

But like, for reals this time.

Listening to podcast after podcast, reading self-improvement books, doing my meditations, getting back in the gym, I could start to see the edges of the picture: happiness, abundance, community, but the finer details were more difficult to imagine. Am I an influencer on social media, or a celebrated and successful adult content producer, or a well-known cam model? Should I continue doing sex work or is there something more I could pursue? Schooling? A trade? Where do I put my focus?

I needed a big picture "why" to guide my actions and give me willpower, and I had lost my big why, lost my feeling of any kind of home, of my routine, my friend group, even the culture I had grown accustomed to.

Coming back to Seattle was never something I wanted, and tried to avoid at all costs, but at some point, I was making other people's lives harder, not just my own by living this way. It felt selfish and badly planned, I lacked the financial foundation to actually do this dream right. The familiar loop started playing in my head. After everything I had put into this? I didn't want to have to give up. It felt like I had failed. Let everybody down, made promises that I couldn't keep.

But with this new clarity I could be less hard on myself. I told myself now I have all the information. I know every step that I must take if I really want to move to Europe one day, specifically France, a much easier target than Switzerland. And the most important thing I would need is to have money saved. $10,000 in my bank account and showing a monthly earning of 2500 Euros per month is basically all it would take. Easy peasy.

Not easy peasy.

The first apartment I moved into had a smell problem so bad that I was sure my upstairs neighbors had murdered someone. The city came and said there was nothing in the code for bad smell, even if it's so horrible and disgusting. It was insufferable coming home to that smell every day, and my building management could not give less of a fuck.

My heat didn't work half the time, it was winter, and when it would turn on it would send loud sputtering water all over the walls and floor. This was not Switzerland anymore and here in Seattle, character meant "old and unmaintained." It was difficult to even be in the apartment let alone stay at home all day and cam. I tried my best to familiarize myself with the local neighborhood and would go on many walks. The Victorian style houses with their perfect and lush gardens, the futuristic and ever-growing skyline of skyscrapers right next to the vintage echoes of a city long gone. Seattle, like its historic buildings, is in need of some serious TLC.

The LGBTQ+ friendly Capitol Hill district of Seattle attracted me with its sexy brown bricks, colorful people and locally owned shops. It had that real PNW hippie vibe, taking me back to the nostalgia of my childhood and providing a placebo effect in place of my lovely Europe. I could walk everywhere and loved checking out all the spots. Here the funk still lived, style, music, and community, here, I could be my eccentric self and not feel so self-conscious.

Or so I thought. Capitol Hill like many of the cities is filled with homeless people and people doing drugs on the street. Safe and at ease are not words I would use while walking through its main areas at any given time of the day but especially at night.

The realization that I can now be randomly shot and that wouldn't be too crazy hits me hard. I'm definitely not in Switzerland anymore. No more assuming the car will stop when you're at a crosswalk because here in America, they will hit you. No more walking alone at night unless you want to be on edge and nervous, white knuckling your pepper spray in your hand the entire time while you maintain the right mix of assertiveness and confidence without bringing too much attention to yourself. No more leaving your purse or drink unattended, no matter what because, well, you never know.

The tradeoff being, I understand this culture, I get the game and dance of the social situations I find myself in. I know mostly what's dangerous and what's not. But it turns out, in comparison to Europe (especially Switzerland) there's a lot more that's dangerous here! We're just fucking used to it!

Walking past fentanyl users with their pants down exposing their assholes is an everyday thing, people covered in dirt and shit and other suspicious substances shooting up in broad daylight at 2pm in a major tourist shopping area in the city, that's just Seattle. We live among poverty and extreme addiction and mental health cases like it's no biggie. You work and if you're lucky you drink at happy hour and on the weekends, you go do something fun. On paper it seems similar to Europe but the energy behind it is completely different.

Europeans always comment on the size of America, and I think now I fully grasp what that means. The sheer size, number of people and districts, it's a massive area that is almost impossible to do completely on foot, or even a bike. I considered upon one of my returns from abroad that I may just use public transportation from now on. Why not?

Well, because it's fucking dangerous. People die on buses here from stabbings. I was greatly discouraged from this idea by my family and ended up keeping my car for the first few months. Until the parking tickets piled so high and unexpected maintenance that would cost $3500 hit me. I chose to take the risk of stabbing over the exploitation of having a car in the city.

The trains and buses overseas make it so easy to do adventures and walk around naturally, the shops are mostly thriving due to all the foot traffic, and it's a lifestyle to be outside as much as possible and cities are designed for humans and not cars. Here it's overwhelming, even just parking your car is on average $250 a month which seems so outrageous to me! But living outside the city means being 100% car reliant, no waking to the shop, or the bodega to get some late-night treats, you will get murdered. It feels so much lonelier in Seattle than in Switzerland, an existential loneliness. Like, I speak the same language as you so why does it feel so hard to relate? I think that's why I fell so hard for this new boyfriend.

I know, I know, but I swear I have *almost* learned my lesson.

It had been over 8 months since I'd completely ended things with Jack. A family member had invited me to a show that one of their friends was playing at. The venue was a historic little bar in the heart of the old part of Seattle, Pioneer Square. His style was groovy and kept me tapping my foot all night, the beer kept flowing and I would find myself chatting with him in the back area until the early hours of the morning. He kept his distance physically but emotionally revealed many vulnerable things about his past and his life.

I am happy that people feel safe around me to tell me their darkest secrets. I've always wanted to be a safe space for people to express themselves without fear of judgment. But there is a pace to things when you're first getting to know someone. I should have clicked that the pace was off. My desire to be seen and accepted as both Lily and Lacy, was strong and I thought maybe someone who's been to the darkness can play in it with me. I thought that maybe this relationship was divine in its timing, and I decided to pursue it further.

However, something in my gut felt off. Was it my past trauma? Was it that I had thick walls built up that I needed to tear down? These questions only made me more curious like he and I were a puzzle to be solved, maybe we each had the key to the others' missing piece.

The first time I visited his place it was dark and crowded, there were crumbs of food littering the entirety of the floor. His bathroom looked like it hadn't been cleaned in years. Maybe I could help him clean this up, I thought. I do love a good before and after and it's easy for me, clearly he needs help.

We had waited some weeks to be intimate. He preferred to just look at my asshole and jerk off, or lick my pussy and jerk off, eventually I started to feel like there wasn't much point in me even being there, I was just a 3D representation of the porn he watched, and it really bothered me. So much so it gave me a panic attack.

Now I know having a panic attack with your partner is a major red flag, but I blamed my trauma and past experiences. I tried to explain why my body was shutting down, why being a sex doll for him to jerk off to was triggering to me. Why it made me feel less than human.

"Can you make love to me?" I asked him.

He looked genuinely confused and afraid and revealed to me that he doesn't think he's ever made love to anyone in his entire life. His biggest fantasy and desire was to do poppers while I fucked him in the ass. I wasn't comfortable with this. I wanted to learn about each other's bodies, souls, and for me starting with drugs was not the way I wanted to establish this intimacy. Not being someone to yuck another's yum I never said no, but asked if we could postpone this particular act.

"Maybe in the future?" I'd say. "When we're more comfortable with each other?"

The more I thought about it though the more I realized he literally could not fulfill any of my intimacy needs, it was always about his boner, and his fantasy, and him feeling uncomfortable with me if I asked for something outside of the porn aesthetic. I tried to give him his fantasy, I played the porn star for him and he loved it, but when I'd ask for sweetness and sensuality in the bedroom his cock would go flaccid.

If I wanted intimacy, passion that built up throughout the day, sweet or sexy messages to build the excitement, if I wanted him to bring the idea (besides me fucking him in the ass on poppers) and it was not me initiating, it would not happen. I got sick of being the one leading the show. What am I a fucking curator for your IRL porn fantasies?

He was an almost 40-year-old struggling musician and a lifelong porn consumer, going on day long porn binges, frequenting bath houses and having unprotected sex with any random stranger because he liked feeling special. He would use his penis pump so frequently that it caused blisters on his dick. He told me about the many STDs he'd acquired while out on his sexual escapades but then assured me this was all in his past. I'm regularly tested, he got tested when we got together. I know I should have seen his stories as warnings, but I felt like if he had a past, maybe I could have a past too?

I was fascinated by this "civilian" who was teaching me things about concepts I had never fully understood from the perspective of the viewer. And as a partner he was giving me everything I thought I wanted. Hungry to grow, appreciative of my opinion and perspective, I watched him change in so many ways right before my eyes. Finally! A partner committed to growth; this is what I had prayed for!

Yet something was missing.

In many ways, I felt sorry for him. If he was a product of the machine I had contributed to, it was my job to fix him, and he made it clear that he desperately wanted me to do so. He made me feel like I was the antidote to all his problems, and being with me was the medicine he needed to get back in the gym, to not live off of frozen pizzas, to finally finish the album he'd been working on for years. I wanted to believe his story; I wanted us to save each other.

I found myself in a constant cycle of breaking up and getting back together with him. I decided to reach out to a somatic sex therapist who was a fan of male anal pleasure. I thought he might be able to bridge this gap in our sex life, maybe I should just fuck him in the ass on poppers? Was it really that big of a deal? What I *actually* learned is that I had no fucking clue how to say no or even recognize where my no began. Maybe this was residue from when I was raped at 15, maybe it was from my years in the porn industry which only rewarded me if I pleased the holy boner, maybe it was from my people pleasing nature, but this therapist helped me find it again.

If I feel that I don't want to be in a relationship, for any fucking reason, I don't have to be. Unfortunately, I felt that feeling and told John that I didn't want to continue forward because I felt we were misaligned and I couldn't give him sexually what he was asking from me, that it was a no. When I came over to have the closure talk, he asked me, "Do you want to go for a walk?"

We decided to keep trying.

My mind was twisting around itself trying to make sense of it. Was this the universe testing me? Seeing if I really have self-respect and not only that but compassion for the other? I was now in the position I had been in before except I was the one pushing him away keeping him at arm's length and he was the one so sure that if he just tries harder, he can show me that he's the one. Two sides of the same ever repeating coin. But now I was in the position of the one who must be honest.

I tried countless times to be done, and each time found myself backing down after we went for a walk and talked. I thought that meant I was seeing the bigger picture, he seemed to be so understanding of the problem, able to verbalize his faults and hurts, but what I'm realizing (through therapy duh) is that when you coerce or convince someone that their wishes are not valid, meaning me wanting to break up, it creates a distrust of the body. So no matter how much the rational mind can twist and flip and create all kinds of narratives of why I should stay in the relationship, my body only stays silent for so long.

Another panic attack. These are really starting to get old.

I'm sitting on the ground, knees to chest trying to explain that I need a moment because my heart is racing, but he doesn't believe me. I tell him I need to go back to my apartment and calm down, I can't continue this conversation in the state I'm in. He won't let me leave because we have to have resolution right then. It was about his sexual needs again and how I made him feel inadequate. I could barely speak, I just wanted to leave but I'd stand and he would block the doorway.

You can't leave like this.

Then let me at least go to sleep and let's talk in the morning.

That answer didn't suffice. We needed to deal with this now, have resolution now, though it had been hours of talking in circles. My body felt weak, my voice tired of explaining, my ego hurt because I felt like I had to soothe his discomfort and mine at the same time.

It was my fault.

His dick would work if I didn't keep bringing up my needs and just gave him a break. It was my fault he had ED, and not his 20 years of overconsumption of porn. I was supposed to be understanding, sex positive. Wasn't I a nice person?

John taught me, however painfully, that I need to trust that adults make their own choices, and that even though he professed to love me so much, my feelings and desires and wants are more than valid, they're the most important.

It's so hard for me to cause pain to others (unless we're getting kinky) and even as a domme I'm not that brutal because I don't deeply love it, I care about the mental and physical well-being of the people I interact with in relationships, but as adults we all have the responsibility to deal with grief in our own ways.

At least that's the relationship coaches say.

My guilt says I'm a terrible person who's walking away from someone who not only accepts but embraces my past. My fucking kryptonite. All I've ever wanted was to be accepted.

But I had to question myself, did he really?

The mirror that he shoved not so gently in my face over and over showed me a sad truth. Was the reason I was choosing all these men and difficult relationships, bouncing all over the world unable to dedicate myself to a goal or path was because it was actually *me* who didn't love and accept myself? Was I in fact still self-harming through these men as a way to right my internalized wrong of being a sex worker? Was I looking for a partner to accept me because in fact, I did not fully accept myself?

Fuck.

In the end I am thankful for what John awakened in me. You see, John was a true fan. Not of me at first but of porn itself. He was a lifelong consumer and knew all the phrases, all the niches and dark alleyways. Not only did he think my job was awesome, he thought I was the coolest and reminded me often that I was Lily fucking LaBeau! International sex superstar respected by her peers and celebrated by her loyal fans.

It's wild how this character of Lily LaBeau has become sentient through the fans who remember me from my scenes. They've created a story about Lily that they want me to roleplay with them over and over on the internet. It seems innocent enough, and on average it is. But there are some days I do not want to be "on" and I don't want to get naked, and I don't want to do my makeup, and I don't want to put toys inside of me. That creates a lot of mental stress when the options are do it anyway, or don't make money that day. Is this a sign that Lily needs to die? Maybe it's time to retire her because as John would often say, "It doesn't really seem like you like this job."

How dare you!

Calling me out with the fucking truth. And what should I do instead? Real Estate? Do I hate sex work? Sometimes. It gets really monotonous, it's always the same fucked up shit, and don't get me wrong, I'm so down to be fucked up and do fucked up shit, it's a glorious taboo embracing act, but the older I get the more I'm just… bored of it. I've done fucked up shit my whole adult life, it feels kinda basic now. Being in love and making love is one thousand million times better than any porn scene I've ever filmed. That's where the real pleasure is, in genuine connection, in safety, in trust, in mutual respect and adoration.

Being fucked up just to be fucked up is just so 2010.

But I can no longer pretend that I'm normal. Right? Because my job is to get naked for guys all day, that should cause some kind of "natural" reaction of jealousy or insecurity in my partner. Right? But like, literally, that's how I make money to live. So what should I do? Do I get a different job that pays a fraction of my current salary and has quadruple the hours? Do I hide my job and with it any hint of my sexuality? Do I hold my partner's hands and help them walk through their insecurity? Do I cut it off and find someone more emotionally mature?

Yes, the answer is D.

Cut it off.

But what about his feelings???

What about mine, bitch? I'm so tired of using others to inflict pain on myself. That's the gross, harsh, painful reality. Maybe they were using me, to feel better about themselves, to punish their mothers, to have a place to cum, but I was using them too. I wanted to pretend that I was just some normal girl because I was so ashamed of being a whore. An unsuccessful whore at that. Yes I made decent money but have never been rich from this industry and yes at times I resented that choice I made to be in porn and the fact that I could not escape it, and the little girl inside me thought if I found someone who would love me that they would save me from my fate.

That's what we're all looking for aren't we? That's the dream of every relationship, isn't it? To save us from our own misery. So I tried to kill this part of myself, over and over, sacrifice it to the conservative gods, and put on my prairie dress to live out the rest of my days with a shameful countenance fixed to my face. I can't tell you how many times I've dreamed about that.

My favorite fantasy is that I have a farm in the woods somewhere near a bit of water, eating off the land, hosting seminars for women. No botox, no facelifts, so synthetic fabrics strangling my pussy, no dildos being shoved inside me unless I wanted them to be, no heavy make-up, gaining weight and feeling zero concern about it. Letting this world go. Surrendering to my humanity.

To get there however, I must be here, living this modern life, thinking in digital ways, looking ahead strategically. I must save money, pay off past debts, and think about the future. And the best way, the fastest way, and the seemingly easiest way would be to double down on sex work and the Lily LaBeau brand. Is this in line with my higher self? Is this the future god would want of me?

Real growth is following what is authentically calling you even when your brain tries to gaslight you and convince you why you don't actually want it. And that's the problem with where I'm at now. I have been gaslit and gaslit myself for years, so I don't even know what the fuck is reality. What do I really want? Is my thirst for new experiences and following my joy and intuition over what "makes sense" actually just a trauma response?

Yet following my joy has given me so much.

It's going to New York to try my hand at professional modeling, it's filming my first porn scene in Miami, it's stepping off the plane and smelling the differences of European air to America's, it's feeling alive and connected when meeting new people in foreign places, it's the satisfaction of finishing a project or task, it's the spontaneous dance off in the kitchen or the unexpected I love you that comes from the deepest part of my heart, it's the pride and satisfaction I feel when I pause and take a minute to look at the world around and really appreciate where I'm at and what it took to get here.

Finally, I'm living in a beautiful and safe apartment, with super-fast high-speed internet. I'm building back up my career and making more money independently than I ever have before because I finally have all the tools I need to do so. This is what I've been working all those hours in therapy for. This is the level up. The only thing standing in the way of my success is daily focus and dedication.

Though sometimes I mess up a step or two, I usually never fall. This is the faith I have created through many years of trial and error. I have cultivated faith in myself, in my ability to work hard and also give myself enough rest, to listen to my body and quiet myself enough to hear my soul. If I don't want to cum for strangers today, that's ok, there's always tomorrow. That's the freedom I have.

This next moment of my life is really about focusing on increasing the workload but getting it more automated and routine, while at the same time focusing on supporting myself with healthy habits like food rest and exercise so I can maintain the longer hours and mental stress.

Do I really want to kill Lily LaBeau?

I mean, sometimes, yeah!

Because the question I've asked myself and have been apprehensive to fully answer is this: is porn a replacement for an abusive boyfriend? It's crossed my mind more than a few times throughout the years. Bold statement and with the fear of alienating my fans one that I believe still may be worthy of a conversation.

Porn as a whole, if you think of it as its own consciousness, has an agenda, and it can't help it. Everyone in porn wants to be the best, but the best in porn language is the sluttiest, the nastiest, the one most able to put the most dicks inside of them, the one who is the biggest lesbian, the kinkiest freak, it exists in extremeness and the pushing of limits, 24/7 horniness.

Be fuckable.

Porn is selling a *fantasy*.

That in itself isn't a bad thing, let porn be porn, let the gooners goon if that's what they choose to do with their life. But I finally had a glimpse of the other side, the consumer experience and the revelation was both inspiring and scary. Yes, to some people porn can become addicting, and when used habitually it damages the sexual competencies of young men.

When you only masturbate and only in a way that's designed to cum as quickly as possible, you're training your body to do that. You're desensitizing yourself to sex with actual humans. That's what scared me, the "hypnosis" of pornography, how the overconsumption combined with conservative propaganda has created a shame machine of epidemic proportions.

Men and women can become lost and confused and detached from their bodies and actual pleasure, imitating porn scenes that they think are the ultimate level of sexual experience. And maybe for some it is! Not trying to yuck anyone's yum, but I am trying to say that it's not everyone's preferred everyday sexual style. I'm saying I'm a porn star and my preferred sexual style is loving, connecting, sensual, with a sliver of kink. As soon as someone starts fucking me like they're in a porn without having the genuine energy behind it, I am immediately turned off.

Extreme doesn't always equal pleasure, and if we're talking pleasure that too can come in so many different forms. Are we talking psychological, physical, sexual, intimate, communal? Pleasure can be received in so many different ways and being the wildest, sluttiest, craziest whore in town has honestly always been way low on my list of things that actually gave me physical pleasure. It was fun, it was novel, it was exciting, it was educational, but full body mind blowing pleasure it was not.

After the first few years it became just work. I would compartmentalize my life; I had my normal personal activities and then with a trusted few I was able to be my porno slutty self. My career became a secret to those I didn't know personally, and I liked having the separation. I thought it was all good.

And then there was John.

He asked me so many questions I had never really considered. I was used to having to hide this side of myself, to not talk about it, to play down my sexiness, you know, so I didn't make my boyfriend insecure. But with John, oh no, he loved all that stuff, he wanted me to dress up more, to wear makeup and heels and he didn't care if they made me taller than him. He wanted to film scenes with me and watch me when I was camming, he was absolutely in love with the sex work lifestyle.

But he couldn't keep a hard on with me if I wasn't in that energy. He too was compartmentalizing me in the opposite way I had done to myself.

It was the elephant in the room. He would tell me of his fantasies he had of performing with me, but we were both routinely disillusioned when reality hit, he physically could not keep an erection during the scene, and this was somehow my fault. I didn't feel safe with him because he couldn't show me sweetness or make love to me as it made him so deeply uncomfortable.

Why didn't I want to bring Lily into the bedroom? Why didn't I want to experiment with toys and different role plays with him that I do with my clients? Why was I uncomfortable wearing lingerie and putting on sexy makeup for him but not for my work? Why did I get mad when I would vent to him about my day on cam and he would become aroused? Isn't that normal for a man? Why was I so insistent on a certain kind of sex and not very open to kinkier experiences? Was I going too far in the direction of prude?

According to my somatic sex therapist, because I don't fucking want to, is enough. I don't have to explain it further. *Like, what?!* That's fucking wild!! I've never thought about it like that. Sad, I know, but hey man, we're all on our different paths. Basically, if it's not a hell yes, it's a hell no, and that's enough. Maybe I do have a bunch of walls up, but in order for them to come down I need to feel safe and being continuously pressured to go out of my comfort zone is not the way to create a safe space.

Porn did fuck me up in some ways. You remember the abusive boyfriend metaphor? Porn taught me that my worth was dependent on my ability to make a man's dick hard and ultimately to get him to cum. That I should basically always be horny and down for whatever because I'm a porn star. That I should love every day and love sex because if I don't that means I probably shouldn't be in the adult industry, "it's not for everyone." That's what people in the industry say and I fucking hate it. I can't just get a normal job, my resume for the past 15 years is sucking dick.

Besides, even if I don't always love it, there are many good days. Are normal people always happy to go to work? Are normal people thrilled to wake up in the morning and make minimum wage to pay some billionaire so he can buy another yacht? We are all in the same fucking mess. We are all slaves to the system. Sex workers have just found another way to survive it.

So fucking what if I don't like my job every day. I still show up and do it, and I do a good job. It has given me more freedom and opportunity than any other person or relationship in my life. Is porn an abusive boyfriend? Only if I choose to let it be. I can say no, I can have boundaries, I can choose to not work when I'm feeling low, I can create safety in my life instead of being a victim of my circumstance, and yes, I know that I have a certain privilege to be able to do that. But after almost two decades, I've put in the time and work to have that privilege.

When I was finally able to get the courage to confess to John (for the umpteenth time) that I no longer wanted to be in relationship with him. He took it way better than I anticipated. We talked for hours, and I tried to be kind but clear, to respect the needs and wants of my body and soul. I told him how much I valued this friendship we had built, and that the last thing I wanted was him out of my life entirely, but as they say, you can't have your cake and eat it too.

"This isn't the first time you've done this. I'm used to it now." A little guilt trip to say goodbye.

Weeks passed with no word, and I started to get angry even though I knew I had no right to be angry. I broke up with him. Couldn't I just leave the poor man alone? But he'd already triggered something in me, insinuating suicide when we'd break up, saying he would never love anyone after me, he made me feel like I couldn't ever be completely out of his life and now he'd gone completely silent. The only thing of his still at my apartment was a guitar he had brought over recently, and it was a reminder every day that things were not entirely finished. I couldn't stand it anymore. Handshaking heart pounding. I texted him simply saying I need to give you your guitar back. Our sentences were no more than 3 to 5 words each, and I felt his anger towards me. I felt like I deserved it, even though he seemed so calm and understanding during our last conversation.

I had images in my head of throwing his guitar out my window, sending him a photo personifying the anger I was feeling. He said he was going to text me about getting his guitar back. Was he just giving me the silent treatment to hurt me? Or was he just hurting?

When I got to his house standing outside his door, like I did so many times I thought my knees were going to buckle. My hands were shaking, and my heart was in my throat. When I saw his face appear in the doorway, I didn't know what to say, but I was angry and sad and disappointed.

Immediately we smiled at each other trying to make the awkwardness fade just a little. I handed him his guitar and then he asked me the question that he's asked me so many times. The question that has always brought us back together after last fights and breakups. The question which I was both afraid of and desperately wanting to hear.

"Do you want to go for a walk?"

I said no.

The Death of Lily LaBeau

Am I the devil? Is Lily evil?

My intentions are pure. To experience life, to explore what's possible with my body and mind. To learn about sex and the many facets of its incarnations. Is that bad? Have I desecrated the temple that is my body or failed to worship it in its true divinity? Can porn not be a form of worship? Is that sacrilegious to even suggest? If God is in everything and we all have a part to contribute to the symphony that is life, can I not be the clearest, truest expression of my own unique note?

Maybe I am possessed. I have been in the fire, witnessed the darker parts of life, been beaten, abused, and questioned my worthiness, my contribution to this world, to my community. Each fire melting me to my core so I can be reborn again and again, wiser, more aligned, more determined.

Have I been lying to myself? Have I been so heavily gaslit by my surroundings that I believe the lies to be of my own creation? Reveling in the seediness and taboo, rebelling against the rules by throwing myself at the imaginary boundaries just to see how far I can go. Hitting my head against the wall that is life so it doesn't forget I'm still fucking here! Am I just a living representation of a trauma response? Unoriginal, blind, a victim to my own fucked up brain and nervous system?

I believe some of us are here to work in the dark, in the places that many are afraid to even look at. In the dark is where the real messy painful bloody growth is created. That's where the most vulnerable, most traumatized, most frightened people, the ones who need the most love and acceptance live… but we also party here. We all have the darkness, some of us just haven't made friends with it yet. Sometimes it feels better not to. Numb. Overstimulated. Better than being afraid, or helpless, or a failure.

When I was younger, I knew I wanted to change the world. I was appalled by the reality that I found myself born into. I knew I was going to do something to change that. I wanted to be a travel writer, my favorite person in the media forever being Anthony Bordain. The kindhearted rebel. He connected people and places like no one ever did before him, he talked to everyone like they were long time friends, he brought attention to worldwide crises and informed without being stuffy or full of himself.

And then he fucking killed himself, and I was so mad at him for that. So mad that he gave up, because the pain of living was too much. His beautiful light just disappeared, without warning. We needed him. Tony, if you're looking down from heaven know that I am still mad at you. And yeah, he's definitely in heaven.

We are all needed in this fight to evolve humanity in a positive direction. Does that include me too? A sex worker? I'm realizing that through all this screaming and crying and begging to be heard and validated, that I was the one who wasn't ok with herself. The sexual side of me, the traumatized side of me, the naive and reckless side of me, the powerful side of me. I have closed down parts of myself and built different walls around my heart for many reasons on and off set. I feel completely inept at managing my life, though somehow seem able to through the grace of sex work. I don't want a normal job. I'm thankful for the freedom and entrepreneurial energy within my field. I get to be creative and my success is my making, which is hard work but so satisfying at the end.

We've lived it Lily ol' gal haven't we? And this body, my body? I love her, I want to be sweeter with her. Scenes are hard and physically demanding, I've been doing this since I was 18. And while I don't hate sex work, I hate feeling like my body is breaking after working non-stop and being treated like a machine and having to smile and look hot through the pain. I hate when I've been on set for 5 hours and my pussy is dry and sore and the shitty lube has long since stopped doing its job, and my mouth, dry from the over exaggerated moans refuses to give me any more spit, but if I stop it will just take longer so I moan louder to drown out my own thoughts and pray they don't ask for a blowjob.

I hate that I almost got 2 awesome jobs that excited me so much and seemed like such opportunities for growth but at the last minute I became too scared to accept because I liked them so much and couldn't handle bringing shame to their company if my coworkers or clients found out that I am still actively in sex work. My face is recognizable, and hiding is not always an option. Everyone's like, just lie. Lie?? Lie about my entire life? All I've ever really done is sex work.

Lily LaBeau

I picked that name because it felt like an old Hollywood starlet, but the meaning has evolved for me over the years. Originally LeBeau I had to change it because an old agent bought the domain name. So I picked LaBeau. An agent would also buy that domain name but at that point I wasn't going to change it again.

La-Beau means "the beauty" but it's grammatically incorrect in French. Beau being the masculine version of the word and "la" being the prefix for a feminine word. And I love that because it's just perfect for me. I feel that androgyny in myself, and I am both parts masculine and feminine. The androgynous beauty, and Lily because it's soft and delicate and magical and quite hard to kill.

She is the wild feminine in me, a passionate and uncontrollable bitch that is so empowered in her sexuality and liberated in her freedom she actually scares grown men with her presence. When I'm deep into my cosplay of "normal" she is the energy that gives away my cover, she puts the crack in my facade, changing my form before their very eyes! I'm not a sweet girl, I'm actually a whore, I'm a slut, I'm a tease, I'm good at it and I love it, and it terrifies them.

She embarrasses me by her choices and lack of restraint. I get jealous of her when having sex with a partner and they want me to "perform" for them. I get angry when I think about how she has contributed to the problems in society, furthering the mass brainwashing of men with her portrayal of the patriarchal wet dream, (even if it was super fun to create). She is the image I can never live up to, always perfectly lit and made-up head to toe, and always, always, horny.

Or at least those are some of the stories I've created throughout the years. The hardest part of writing this book was figuring out where the end was. What was the lesson? The big grand finale of all the trials and tribulations? What beautiful wisdom will I feed my audience, what taste will I leave lingering in their mouths? I began writing this in 2017, and kept thinking I had found my happy ending only to be repeatedly disappointed each time I realized the situation I found myself in was not my castle, my prince, or even my fairytale, wondering when will I finally get my happy ending? This surely is where I fade off into the sunset.

It was not.

Even if I'm not still 15 and cutting myself I am still self-harming by not prioritizing my life, my health, my happiness. Beating myself up and focusing on the fear and not the many blessings I have right now. This lingering moral guilt, this pervasive question, do I really like this job? Are my body, mind and soul aligned and consenting to me being a sex worker? Why am I constantly escaping from success, which feels right there at my fingertips.

Life security. I want it!

Haven't I redeemed myself enough? What about all the fans that tell me that I've saved them from difficult times in their lives, accompanied them through their periods of depression and isolation? Or the ones that tell me I've given them the inspiration and courage to live the life they dreamed? The ones that tell me I'm what they look forward to after a long week. The ones that trust me with the secrets they've never told anyone before? Is that not real? Is that not valid? Don't I get any brownie points for that?

Why does it seem like other girls love this so much more than me? Why do they still feel libido and excitement for sex when I feel anxiety and fear when I have to interact with a man who's not a porn star? I've felt like an imposter since day 1, trying to prove that I belong and in the end it didn't even matter. No one's approval will pay your rent, this became a career because I was good at it and know how to make money doing it. It literally doesn't fucking matter if I like it or not.

The real question is: Do I feel like I'm valid? Like really in my heart and bones do I believe what I do is not only legitimate but also important for the world? Do I take myself and my career as seriously as I could or am I perpetually one step in one step out, like a bad relationship. What exactly am I running from?

Maybe it's the Groundhog Day repetitive cycle of dick ratings and jerk of instructions, the oohs and ahhh so perfected I sound exactly like the girls I made fun of before doing this for so long. Somedays I feel like I've become an empty sex robot, on autopilot because most men's fantasies are pretty basic and fucking boring and the ones that are actually exciting make me question my own morals and feelings about performing them. At least it's something new?

Maybe I do like it. Being a whore on camera. Somedays I fucking love it, and I'm ashamed of that. Internalized whorephobia. It conflicts with my idea of perfection; the good girl programming so deeply embedded in me it's literally causing me to short circuit. According to the statistics, I'll never have a man at this point, based on my height, age, education and of course, my decades long porn career. So why quit? The damage is done.

This is my destiny. I just haven't quite figured out why. Or why I need to figure it out. Why do I feel like I have to show the world that I'm strong enough and smart enough to make a success out of this life? To prove I'm not another statistic?

Well guess what. I am. I'm a traumatized girl with daddy issues that was raped when she was 15 and suffered with self-harm who turned to porn for validation and fame. Does that mean my experience isn't valid? Is that not the narrative I'm supposed to reveal? I'm also the girl that fought year after year to learn, to grow, to explore, to create and who never gave up. Porn shaped me and taught me the hard way, but I learned. It doesn't matter how or why I got into this business, what matters is that I am and I have to deal with the same stigma that everyone else does. I recognize my privilege, and I also recognize the struggle.

The world wants to pretend that they want to help us but what would that actually look like?

Decriminalization.

Social Acceptance.

Seeing us as human, just like you.

We are all dealing with our own struggles and sex work is a way we've learned to make money. If people really want to save us, they need to make it safe for us to do that, not take away our freedom or ability to work.

There's this thing called the Karpman drama triangle. Basically, there are 3 roles that are continuously stuck in a drama loop, and they are the Victim, the Prosecutor, and the Rescuer. For so long I was in the rescuer role and then feeling rejected when someone no longer wanted me to rescue them. I think the world is also often stuck in this drama cycle, wanting to rescue sex workers thus making us into the victim.

The only person who has to live with the consequences of my choices is me. Almost every fucking day I'm reminded, if not by myself and my circumstances then by others and their reactions. Every day is like navigating Thanksgiving with your toxic family. Say enough, don't say too much. Be friendly but not annoying, ask questions but don't go too deep or they will ask you more, try not to lie just avoid the question. It's exhausting.

Just be honest.

Honesty is not the magic solution and ends up messing things up more than it helps. There are too many shame filters, too much cultural apathy towards sex workers. We need more honest conversations to humanize people in the sex industry but there are so many PR stunts, marketing ploys, and content that just drives the same mainstream narrative of porn and sex work. It's career suicide to break the fourth wall especially in porn. There is always a facade, even realness is a genre.

The point is, there is nothing wrong with each individual's expression of sexuality as long as it is consensual. The world has been trying to tell me all the things that make me "bad" my entire life, but I did consent at the time to all the things I did. I used to think beating myself up for every accident and misstep somehow kept me moral, that I had to feel horrible for not being perfect.

After years of being the public scapegoat I've started rejecting the projections of other's shame onto me. Then I was able to see my shame more clearly. My lifestyle may conflict with the beliefs of others, but it is my life to live, and others shame is not mine to carry. My challenge is to remain authentic to my wants, desires, and personal boundaries, and if possible, to inspire through my actions that there are many ways to live one's life.

Any man who loves me will love me regardless of my work.

I still believe that. And I also believe that the men I dated didn't actually love me, they loved the idea of me, the fantasy, and I loved being that fantasy, too afraid to be my authentic self. Yes, I used porn as a way to cope with my autonomy being taken away when I was a teenager, and porn also gave me a space where I could express my sexuality within the confines of rules and professional boundaries. Through that I slowly learned that even off set I should have the same autonomy and ability to speak up for myself. It was a hard way to learn, but it did give me the lessons I needed to learn. I got my no back.

This business is not for everyone. Sex work can take you to very dark places and it's not the only path to learning deep truths, but it sure is a quick and dirty one. Sadly, it's also a make or break route, and has taken beautiful souls away from us. I do not say this lightly. Being in the sex industry can give you the deepest understanding of yourself through cultivating your own lived truth, or it can kill you. This path can be so hard and lonely and ostracizing and can facilitate a furthering of trauma and mental and physical abuse.

If you learn to master boundaries, you learn to master your life and your happiness. You don't have to be ok with everything and it's just as important to know what you don't like as it is to discover what you really do. There are bad actors in the world, mistakes will be made, bad things will happen, learning to navigate these moments and mitigate future risk once new information is obtained is literally the whole point of life.

The more you "fail" the more you learn, and after you dust yourself off, you gotta try again. It's painful being alive, it's a horrible feeling to have your heart broken, to lose a loved one, to witness people and children starving and being murdered, and all the other circumstances that make our hearts sink to the floor. Betrayal, manipulation, paranoia, anxiety, depression, social situations, financial stress, hopes and dreams smashed in front of your face, life can be a fucking cock sucking bitch. A real mother fucking piece of shit. A dumpster storm of radioactive bugs just flying at your face and getting stuck in your hair and mouth as you're screaming No! Stop!!! Please! Have mercy!! Yes, life can feel like a senseless, cruel, and decaying lump of rock with a bunch of real fucked up entitled assholes destroying it.

I know.

But we gotta see it through 'til the end.

Because in between the shit show, is the best dinner you've ever had, the one where you can't stop laughing with some of your closest friends. It's the top of the mountain after a long hike. It's the sweet treats, delicious smells, and beautiful music that send your heart to another time, another place, a happy moment. I still don't have all the answers, I can't tell you what happens when we die, or how you can make $20,000 a month on Only Fans selling feet pics. But I can tell you with absolute certainty that there is good in the world. Most of the people I talk to online are not horrible people, they are generally respectful, shy, lonely, and just looking to feel good for a moment. That's not a sin.

Hating ourselves, compartmentalizing every part that feels scary, or dark, or wrong is what is killing us.

It's ok to be a paradox. You're not a computer program; you don't have to make sense. I'm a porn star that likes to cuddle more than fuck, my favorite position is missionary and I'm pretty much over sex after about 10 minutes. I hate facials, and will never squirt for you, my preferred dick size is about 6 inches and would rather make love than fuck any day of the week. I like dressing up and looking pretty but because my job requires me to be in full makeup and sexy outfits all the time, my favorite thing to wear is sweatpants, a baggy shirt and no makeup. Sexually I've done so many crazy acts and the thing that turns me on the most is making out with the person I love.

Screw the stereotypes, live your fucking life!

Stop cosplaying, start embodying.

I'm yelling at myself. Life seems to give you what you need when you're ready for it. Of course, you never feel ready for it when it happens. I am a baby who is constantly humbled by the lessons I go through. Preemptively feeling the desire to harden up and brace for impact at all hours of the day, waiting for the invisible hand to strike, and when it inevitably does, it hurts.

Can I soften after the blow, let go, and reconnect to myself, my morals and my sovereignty? When the shame is constricting my whole body like a giant snake, can I surrender again and again into its embrace, letting it grow tired and slither away? I want to fight! To prove them all wrong! But the challenge is to surrender, to soften, to allow loving energy back into my heart and body.

I have worked to build my brand, shot over 500 scenes in my career and have hundreds of millions of views on tube sites. I get stopped in the street by people who know and love me, and I have amassed hundreds of thousands of fans on my social media profiles. Which, for social media these days is not that huge but still it's a testament to the work and energy I have put into building Lily LaBeau. And this persona has formed a digital life all of her own.

For so long I tried to find ways to play down my porn persona. It's like I wanted a trophy for being "just a normal girl" outside of my work. I wanted to be digestible, and palatable for others and even to myself. I don't know what I was trying to prove. Being isolated from the tribe called "mainstream world" feels shitty, not feeling like I truly belong to the tribe called porn is disheartening, but being inauthentic to myself feels shittier. I don't want to be normal, just for a little bit I want to be her again. Naive. Excited. Stars in her eyes.

So I called Mark Spiegler and asked him if I could come back. He declined. So then I asked Twitter and was given the number of a new agency and made plans to go to AVN and meet with them and make the rounds with directors and get back in the business.

Going solo into the desert of Las Vegas to complete my job signing at a company's booth for AVN was a surreal moment. There were so many faces I knew from before, and the convention turned out to be pretty fun. So many lifelong fans and industry people that I used to work with stopped by the booth I was at and reminisced with me about fond memories. I felt happy, and included, I was excited when discussing coming back and doing girl on girl only scenes for different directors. Looking around at the half naked girls and various sex objects and dildos I just thought, I love this shit.

However, there was a small problem.

Lily LaBeau is dead.

I thought she'd reappear at the convention and though I smiled and went through all the motions, she was nowhere to be found. I thought that she would be happy to be back with me and our little porn family. I mean I know I've been mulling over the idea of murder this entire book, but I changed my mind! I do love her! I was just being an asshole and blaming her for all my problems in life. Maybe it was this last declaration of my hatred for her that was the final straw?

I guess if we love someone and they say they hate us and wish we were dead, we'd walk away from that person too. I know she loves me and has always been there to protect and support me, but no matter how many times I said I wish she was dead I never thought I would have to face the world without her, just me, Lacy.

Lacy is self-conscious of her belly rolls and dry skin and wrinkles, and cares about what other people think and prefers to hide behind big glasses than be all dolled up and glamorous. She hates uncomfortable clothing and being cold, inefficiency and things being harder than they need to be. There's always something that can be cleaned before the space feels ready to shoot. Lacy loves a good relaxing clutter free ambiance and especially the feeling of the sun as it illuminates her little apartment, she does not want to turn on the studio lights and shut the blinds. Smoking weed every day waiting for inspiration for working to strike while spiraling into my own hazy cloud of disassociation, writing the letter apologizing to my fans that their customs are late over and over again but not actually typing or sending it.

Clearly, I haven't found the magic solution yet. I haven't fallen in love with the man of my dreams. I haven't mastered a healthy lifestyle or found monumental success in my career. I'm scheduled to go do scenes in LA in less than a month. I have 2 weeks until I am forced to move out of this condo as the owners are selling and must again pack up or sell off my life. On to the next book. This book is done. I always thought that the end would be profound and overwhelmingly joyful and full of celebration. She did it! She's so successful!

Sorry.

The meaning of life is to live. That's it. Sometimes things flow, sometimes they don't. Sometimes people will be horrible, sometimes you're the little piece of shit. That's ok, because we just keep trying to be better. Am I ever going to be a mega famous superstar porn babe with her own meme? Probably not. Can I save up money over the next few years and invest in my older self's quality of life by being smart now? Fuck yeah, I can. People are right, I can't do porn forever, but I just turned 35 years old, I think I've got a few years of fuckability left in me, at least.

The final lesson that will make it in this book might be the most important, and also the most painful and disheartening and soul crushing and that is, when someone repeatedly treats you badly, they should not remain in your life. Over and over, I can see the pattern with the men I date: charming, nice guy, but actually low-key resents and hates me, and shows it in passive aggressive ways and not that funny jokes. I've literally been dating the toxic parts of myself, the toxic parts of my family, my parents, my sibling. I've been seeking love through such a distorted lens, of course I hated myself.

But when I was left with only myself, I had to become my friend. I had to put my needs first, my grief first, but also my joy. It was liberating! And powerful in a way which I've never felt. Spoiler alert. Your needs matter. And mine. And it's ok to want a safe life, with safe people. And together we are inhabiting this sick world, with sick ideals, and sick culture. That makes this harder, but there is a revolution going on and we cannot escape it nor should we want to. Disillusionment can feel like a face plant to concrete, the embarrassment, the guilt, the shame. The revolution is the aftercare, the people who give you tissues and clean up your bloody nose, who feed you and clothe you, who hold and remind you why you're loved when you are feeling fragile.

Lily hasn't come back, and if you haven't gotten the metaphor by now, that means the mask is gone. I have become too real and, in the process, shattered the thing I made to hide behind, and it's never coming back, she's never coming back. She was my shadow, my power and protector, my mother, my friend. I've become that for myself. Lily LaBeau is embedded in everything, in every interaction, her legacy is plastered on my face, where it belongs.

I wear it with pride and reverence. Yes, I'm still making sexy content, and I'm still doing scenes in Los Angeles, and I feel fine about it. Not overjoyed, not sad and victimized, simply going over the logistics in my head and on paper. I can finally say I enjoy my work, and I love creating really hot adult content, for now the cost is worth the reward, though I'm still exploring other avenues of creating to prepare for the potentiality of adult entertainment being made illegal.

I am an actress, a performer, and an entertainer. That's what I love to do, and it gives me a lot of internal satisfaction. Balance is everything though, with working and a personal life and extracurricular activities, I must be strict yet flexible with my activities and schedules. I'm a real adult now, this barely legal teen is now in her mid-thirties. It's chill though. Traveling every other month to LA seemed daunting at the beginning but I'm finding my rhythm, and I've got good people around me, I shake off the missteps and roll with the punches. It feels good to be my own center of gravity and not so easily swayed by the whims of the external world.

The scenes have been super hot, and I'm tapping into my own personal flavor of sensuality and eroticism while performing and after a few weeks decided to start doing BG scenes again, because I wanted to. Looks like baby bird still knows a few tricks! I had a nice long chat with my somatic sex coach and realized doing a great scene, is just a matter of knowing what questions to ask the other performer beforehand, to flirt, tell them how you like to be fucked. Communication is sexy.

Did we have this much consent talk when I was in the biz? I don't think so, the industry has evolved a lot. Talking to new performers and just being there on each other's journeys, it's a really special feeling. Doing scenes together is always a unique dance that, like dancing, is terrifying when your partner doesn't know the steps and so rewarding when you're all in sync. But that's the work. Paying attention and responding.

Not only that, the people that I've met in the industry bring me so much joy. Returning to set was like a sweet homecoming, and I couldn't have felt more adored and respected than I did on my last trip. They love me, they really do, and I love them too. I'm not sure if porn is the source of all the problems in the world or the symptom and I don't think I'll ever fit in with "normal" world and honestly, I still don't feel like I fully fit into the porn world. And I don't actually give a fuck. My personality and way of being is going to be triggering and annoying to some people but that's not my fucking problem.

We all wear different masks at different times. The cold and sexy siren, the perfect pristine bombshell, the nympho housewife, the not-so-innocent young girl, the freaky book nerd… the list goes on and on. Yours might be, the movie buff, the one who never gets laid, the gooner, the incel, the nice guy, the player, the faithful partner, the rebel without a cause.

Masks can be used for so many different reasons and sometimes for a while they serve a worthy purpose, they're not all bad, as long as you don't forget you're wearing them. At our essence, our cores, our souls, we are made of love. We just wake up every day and forget that. God, the universe, it's made up of love. It is faceless and formless and infinite and powerful, and it animates all of us.

You're like, wait, so you're saying everyone in the industry wears masks? To some extent, well, yeah, it's literally the job and there's no shame in that. Though I do believe some creators find literal holy communion through the stuff they shoot. They're the ones that are tapped 24/7 into the erotic, and that's so awesome! Some find erotic in the unusual, the not so straightforward taboo elements, the more shadowy and psychological side of the erotic. Doing porn can be sexually satisfying, but it doesn't satiate my deep erotic hunger. Which feels primal but, more connective, more explorative and playful.

Choosing to love myself, choosing to trust God and trust in the divine timing of my path and my destiny, choosing to continue the healing path even after what feels like endless failed attempts, is choosing *faith*. That fucking babe. Faith that there is love out there for me, in community, in life, and in a partner. Faith that I can accomplish what I've dreamed about my whole life, even with every little side quest and bonus adventure in between. Faith that in the end we are all specs of dust on the magnificent tapestry of the universe and there are a billion things we will never understand about what it means to be humans living on planet earth so why not madly follow that which gives us life, that which animates us. Why not follow love?

That means no hating yourself or hating others for their choices.

Continuing in sex work means there will be more bouts of BV and yeast infections, there will be annoying days on set and disappointing moments, there will be awkward first dates and cringeworthy introductions with strangers, but this time whenever I go back home, I'm going back one step closer to the life of my dreams. When the scene is over, the act is over. I get to be me, and be sexy the way I feel most comfortable, in my sweatpants and a baggy t-shirt, no makeup, doing something I love, AND feel absolutely zero fucking guilt or shame about any of it. That's the game changer.

I've been at war with myself and I have used Lily as an excuse and a way to blame something or someone else. Life is hard, we make mistakes, we learn hard lessons, we are victimized, abused, and then asked to keep our hearts open. I'm not saying I deserved mistreatment, but in this lifetime, I believe porn gave me the lessons I needed to grow and understand my family and personal trauma and to overcome it. I'm lucky, but I'm also privileged and blessed. There are many factors at work in my evolution and success and I don't take all the credit, but I do take some. My life is in my hands and if I wanted it to change, I had to do my part to change it.

The thing is, at this point, I fully believe in my ability to reach my goals and porn is a tool, one I'm very thankful to have at my disposal. Therapy is a tool, and I am also so thankful for that. Sex work gives me freedom to shoot all over the world, make my own schedule, and create cool stuff, and I am incredibly thankful to be able to do that.

If the cost is not fitting in everywhere with everyone, so be it. Life is too short to wait to go after your dreams. And I've been waiting for over a decade. I always knew that one day I would feel it was time, to stop constantly being on the go, to put down roots, to be successful in my career, and being at peace with myself. I knew one day I'd grow up, and I think I'm like 40% of the way there. Finishing this book will increase the score by 5%. It's my story and it's my prayer for my future as well.

I have a clear vision guiding me and my actions, and my values and priorities are easy to see rippling throughout my life. I am not only in the driver's seat, I've customized the whole car to be the coolest and most awesomely efficient possible. It's not hard to love me, it's hard to love a fake version of me.

No more apologizing for not fitting into anyone's limited idea of what I should be, not even my own. Porn is never going to be the conversation around the dinner table, I'm not going to change the world today, perfection is a fucking illusion, and the greatest source of passion and pleasure comes from my heart, then pussy. I may dream of a utopian world, but I have no clue how to go about achieving that. I want everyone to be free and I believe the worst chains are the ones we put on ourselves and if we truly want to help others, we must release our own bondage first.

Meet our needs first.

And wouldn't you know it? In the last year everything has changed. My mom is buying 5 acres of farmland in northern Washington and has asked me to manage it and host retreats and classes and plan the crops. My dream is finally happening, but I couldn't do it on my own. I'm so ready and excited for this project with my mom and we've been working hard for years to create safety, trust, and respect in our relationship.

I've also been working closely with a company in Switzerland called "Let's Share", a strap-on sex toy with a vibrator attachment on the side of the wearer that responds to the rhythm and motion as you pleasure your partner. I invested in the company because I thought it was an ingenious product that created more shared pleasure for both parties and is inclusive to all bodies and preferences. What more could you ask for in a sex toy? They said they could offer me a work visa in Switzerland next year as a social media manager once we build up revenue for the project, but at this point, I don't know if I'm ready to move again. I feel like I'm finally ready to stop running. I'm finally happy with where I'm at right now.

I've had a few short-term boyfriends since the last one ended but now clearer in my expectations and boundaries, I ended things early on when I noticed red flags. Go me!! Of course I'd love a partner, but never again do I want to sacrifice my own mental and physical health to have one.

I also have found a small community of amazing sex positive people here in Seattle. We meet up regularly, sometimes to shoot sexy content, sometimes just to watch movies. I can be myself with them, and they seem to genuinely like me too.

I've been working hard on my sobriety and haven't smoked weed since the first of the year. I promised myself one year free of weed and the farther on this path I go the more I feel like I don't need it anymore. I have healthy coping skills now, I'm kind to myself, I let go of toxic relationships, and I take care of my body and my mind.

Is this growing up?

Well, I'm not quite there yet but I can see where I'm going very clearly. I have a vision I hold in my mind every night and I feel I'm getting closer and closer…

Every day I wake up to the sounds of birds and the smell of forest, I look at my beautiful home and have so much gratitude for my life and the security I feel. I roll over and snuggle up a few more seconds with my partner whom I love so deeply and then get up and start my morning routine, being present with each part, each new bud, each new flower, being present in my life. I am calm, my work is successful, and I have many sources of income. I find so much joy and purpose in the retreats I host at my home. My mother is safe and happy and bakes bread for the guests. My sister and nieces and nephew visit often and help out with the land enjoying sunshine filled days and fresh fruit picked right off the branch. I have so much abundance, so many resources and healthy ways of serving people. My family is taken care of and secure and my community is thriving and vibrant with growth and ideas and action plans. I have healed my relationship with money, with my past, and the way I relate to the world. I feel so loved and connected to others. There's talk of marriage and babies in the air, and I can feel myself excited for this next chapter of my life. I look back on the journey so far, now wisdom, and I am so thankful for every moment. As I walk through my gardens and feel the morning light kissing my face, smell the fresh dew on the grass and feel the warmth of the cup of coffee in my hands, I am happy.

Epilogue

My gift is death.

I am a phoenix, and my gift is death. Through every death I am reborn, over and over and over, each time my plumes gaining more color, more shimmer, more dimension. My tears are magic, and they water the earth with the truth of the achingly beautiful sadness that comes with being alive. I walk on the ground, I am comfortable in the grass, but my home and where I feel most alive is flying in the sky.

I have no clue how many lives I have left, or how long I can continue this cycle of being burned alive and growing out of the ashes of my past self. It's uncomfortable, it's painful, unsettling, I resist, I protest, and yet surrendering to the flames is the only way to survive.

I still fear death, the moment when I realize it's truly my end. I still fear not having all the answers, not doing enough with the gift that is this incredible life. I can't explain the atrocities and horrors of life, or how to fix the homeless crisis or stop the world from dropping nuclear bombs all over itself.

All I can do, my gift and my power, is to be unapologetically myself and hopefully inspire you to do the same. I am a magical creature, but I am not the only one, and right now our magic is not only needed, it's necessary. We have to offer the hand we were never given, we have to pull each other up together, we have to take back our power, individually and collectively, and in this current climate we are all hoping for a miracle because that's what it seems it will take.

You and I are so much more powerful than we can even imagine, so stop fucking beating yourself up. Stop making excuses for why everyone else deserves to be happy but not you. That's fucking bullshit and you know it. Stop letting other people's fear dictate your life, these are not your stories, these are remnants of a world that is dying, that must die, so that we can be reborn into the new one.

The world needs you, needs me, whole, focused, embodied. I can't save the world, but I hope I can inspire you to save yourself. You belong here, you are worthy, whether you're a snake, a bird, a badger or a water buffalo, you are exactly who you need to be. It's time to own it and stop looking at everyone else for permission.

Lily LaBeau had to die, if only so that she could be reborn, and to give Lacy the chance to decide if she truly wanted to go on living because there were many times I wasn't sure. These two sides both needed to go into the darkness and when they reemerged together, they were finally united. Dark and light, material and immaterial, unashamed, empowered, emboldened, the chips on my soul now healed with gold, the anger in me now a force guiding me to make the changes that are needed instead of directing the harm to myself.

I can't promise you I will live a long life, my lungs still taste of ash, in my body chemicals and poisons float along their way, my mind and brain permanently damaged after years of abuse and neglect. My only purpose for now is to live, genuine, authentically. One day I will die a final and lasting death, as this is the fate of us all as, but as long as there is breath in my body, and hope in my heart, I promise, I'm not going anywhere. I'm here, with you, to fight until the very end.

Fight for love.

Fight for life.

Fight for healing.

Fight for justice.

This book, this beginning part of my life is complete, but my legacy and my destiny is just getting started.

Vive LaBeau.

Go Fund Me Page for Sarah Shevon:

https://www.gofundme.com/f/ulcerative-colitis-surgeries-care-expenses

Check Out Let's Share on Instagram : @lets_share_community